GLOWING MANDALAS

LIN WATCHORN

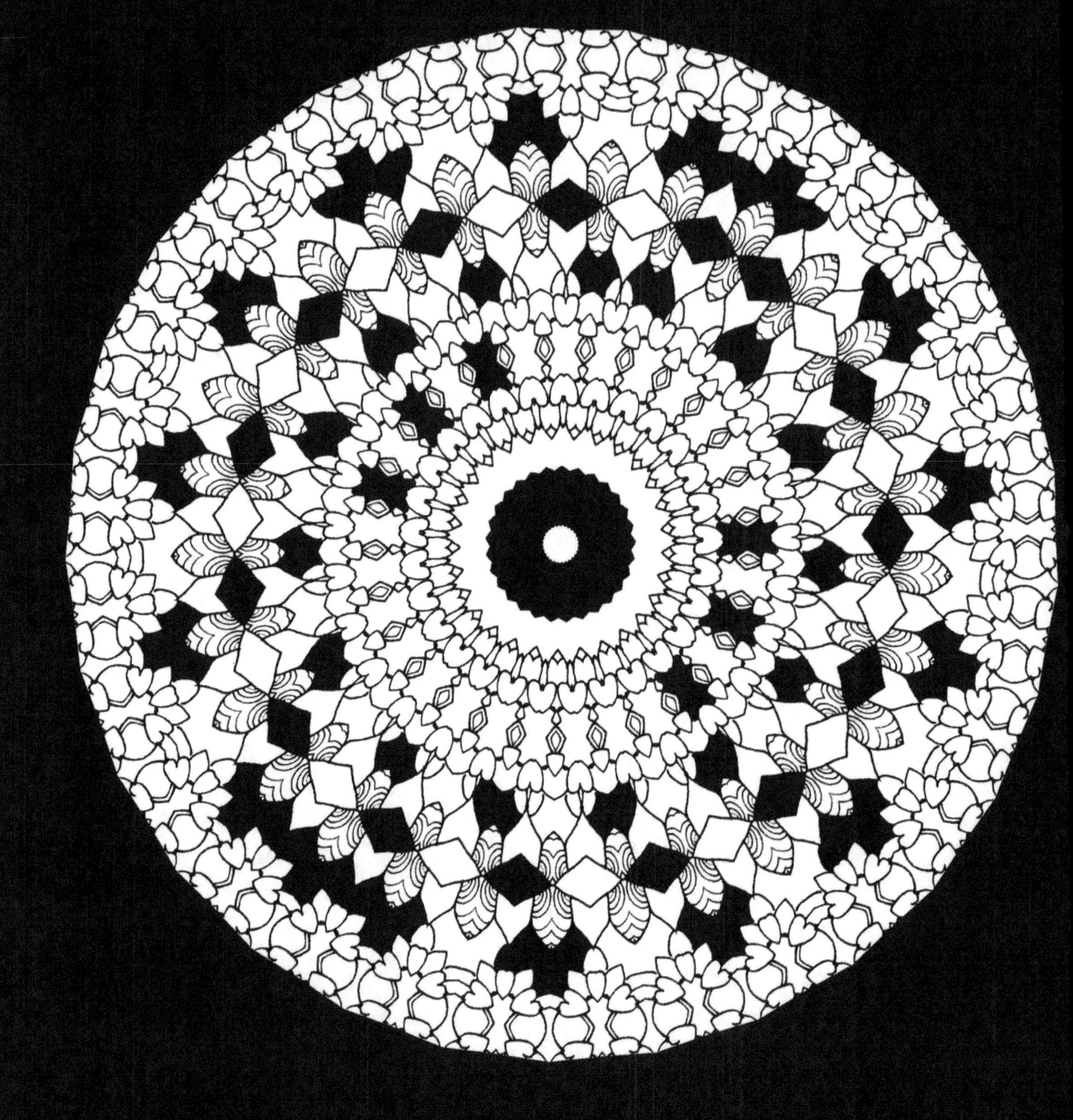

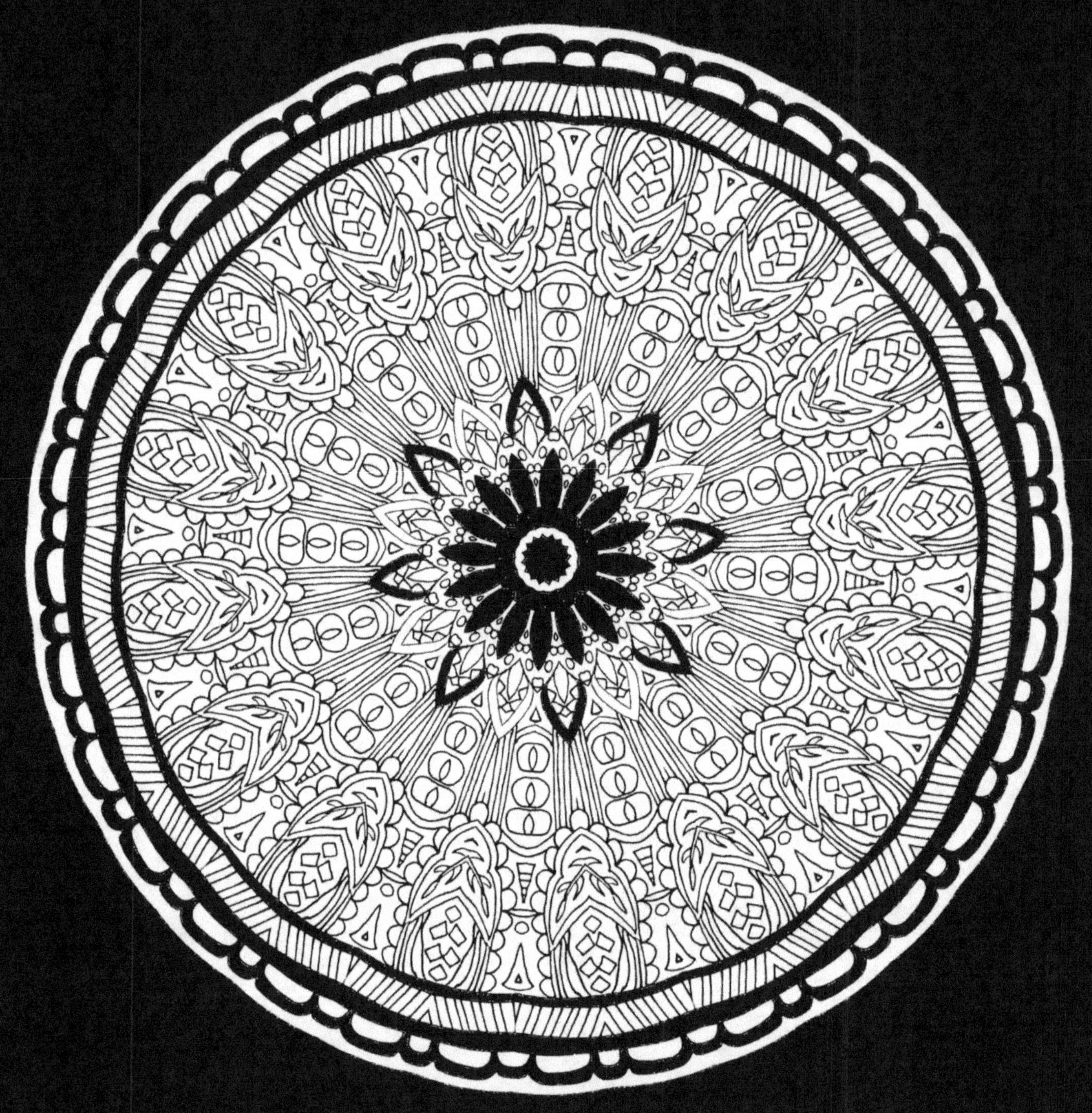

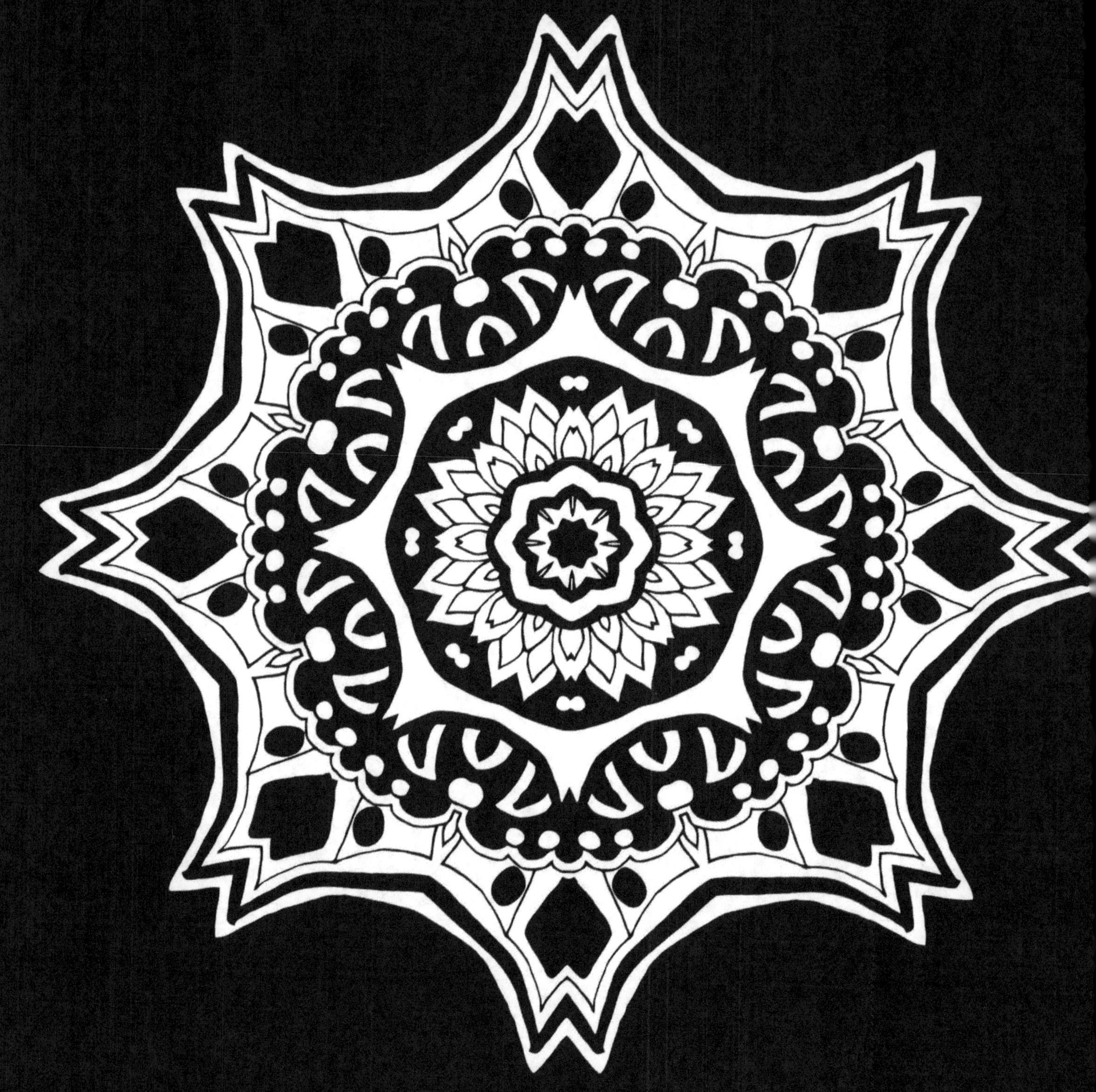

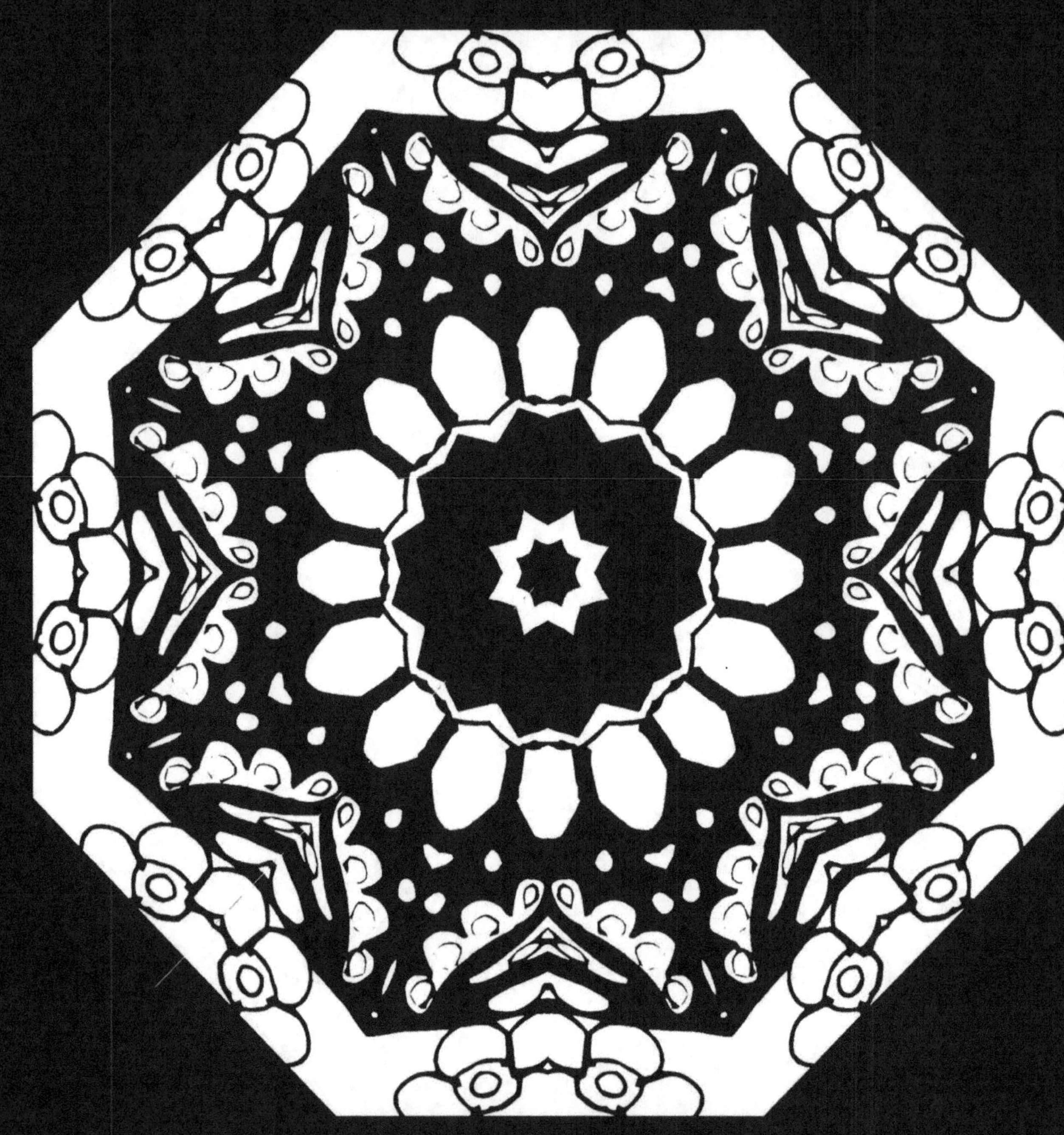

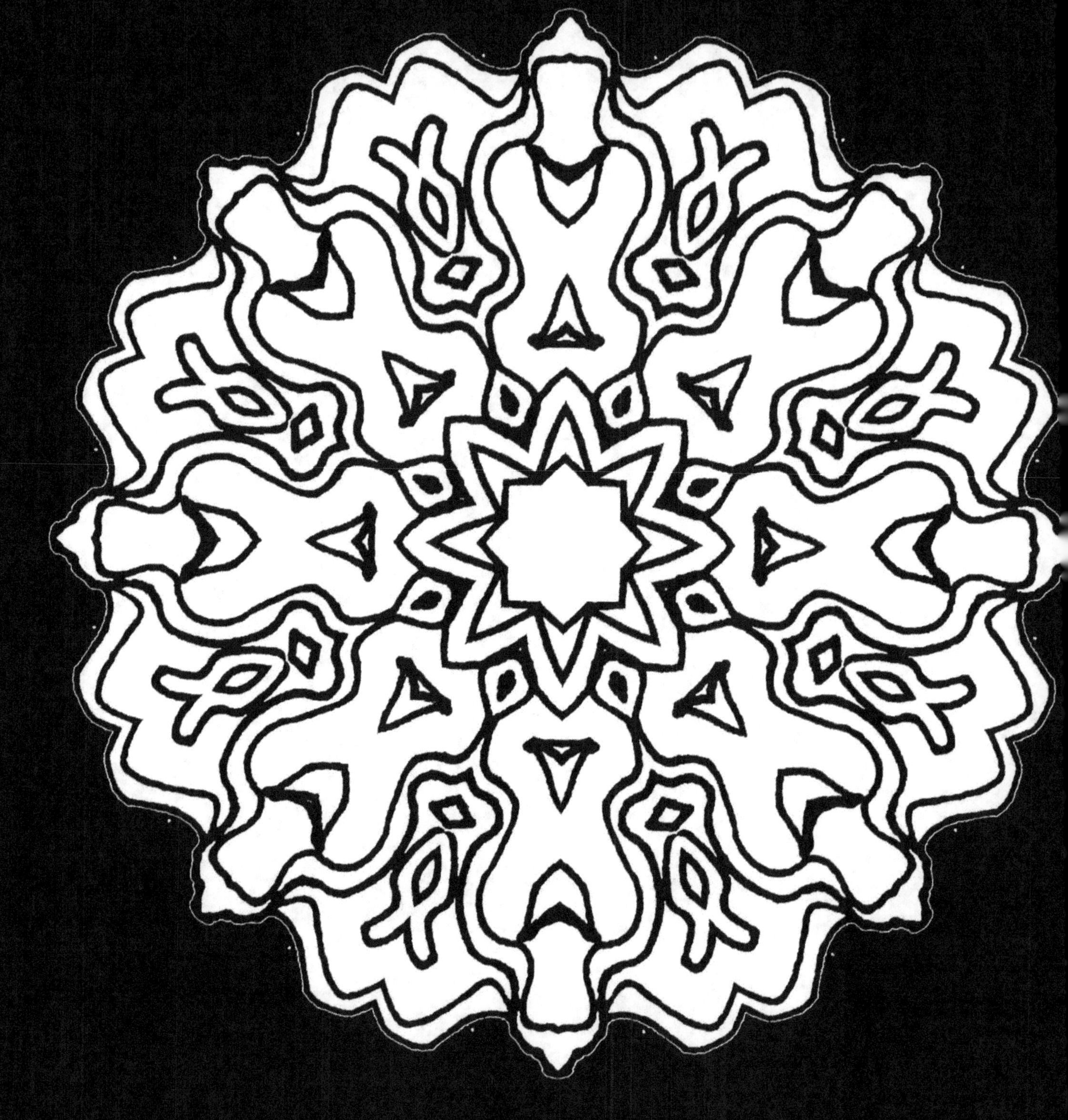

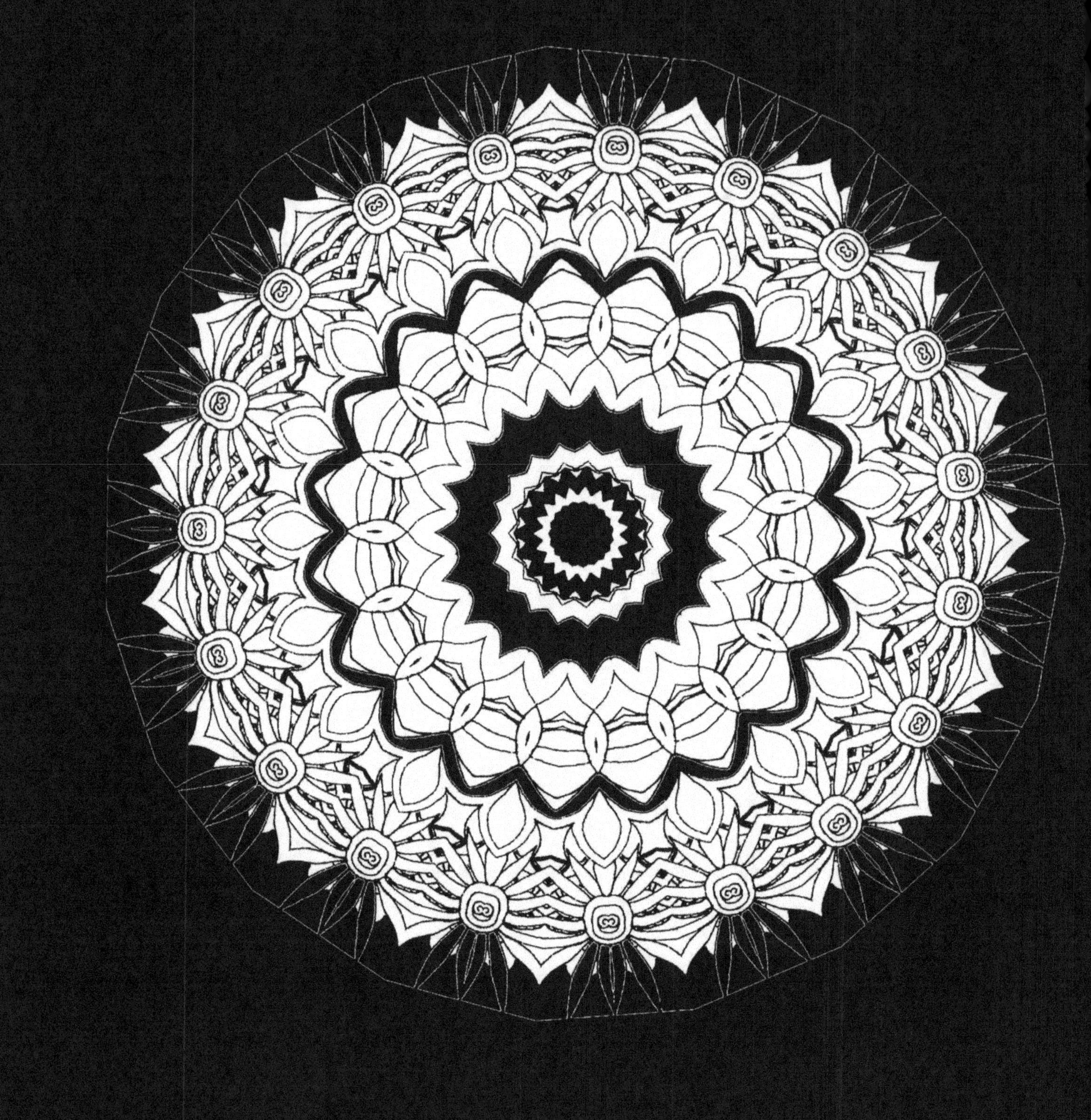

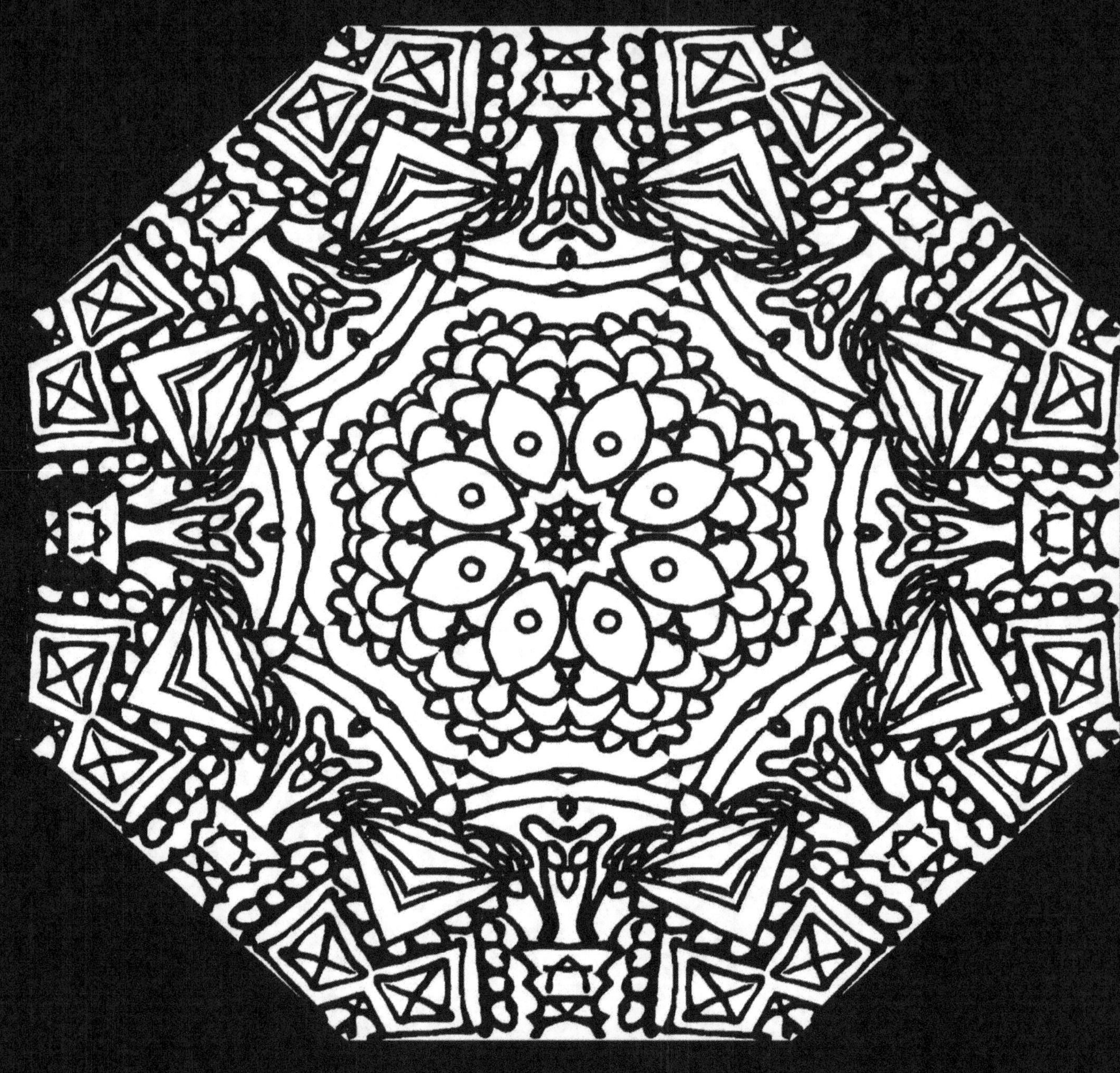

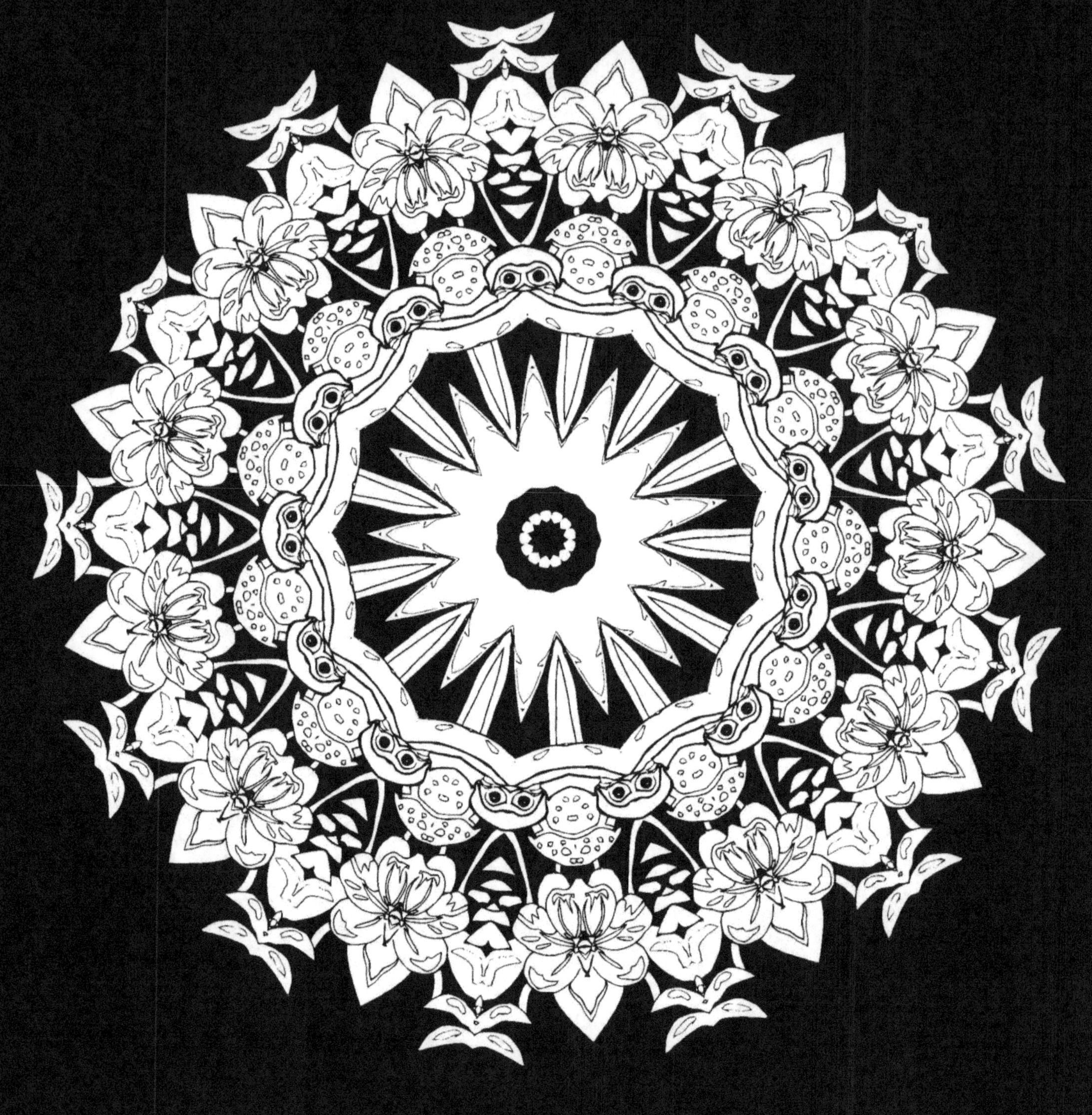

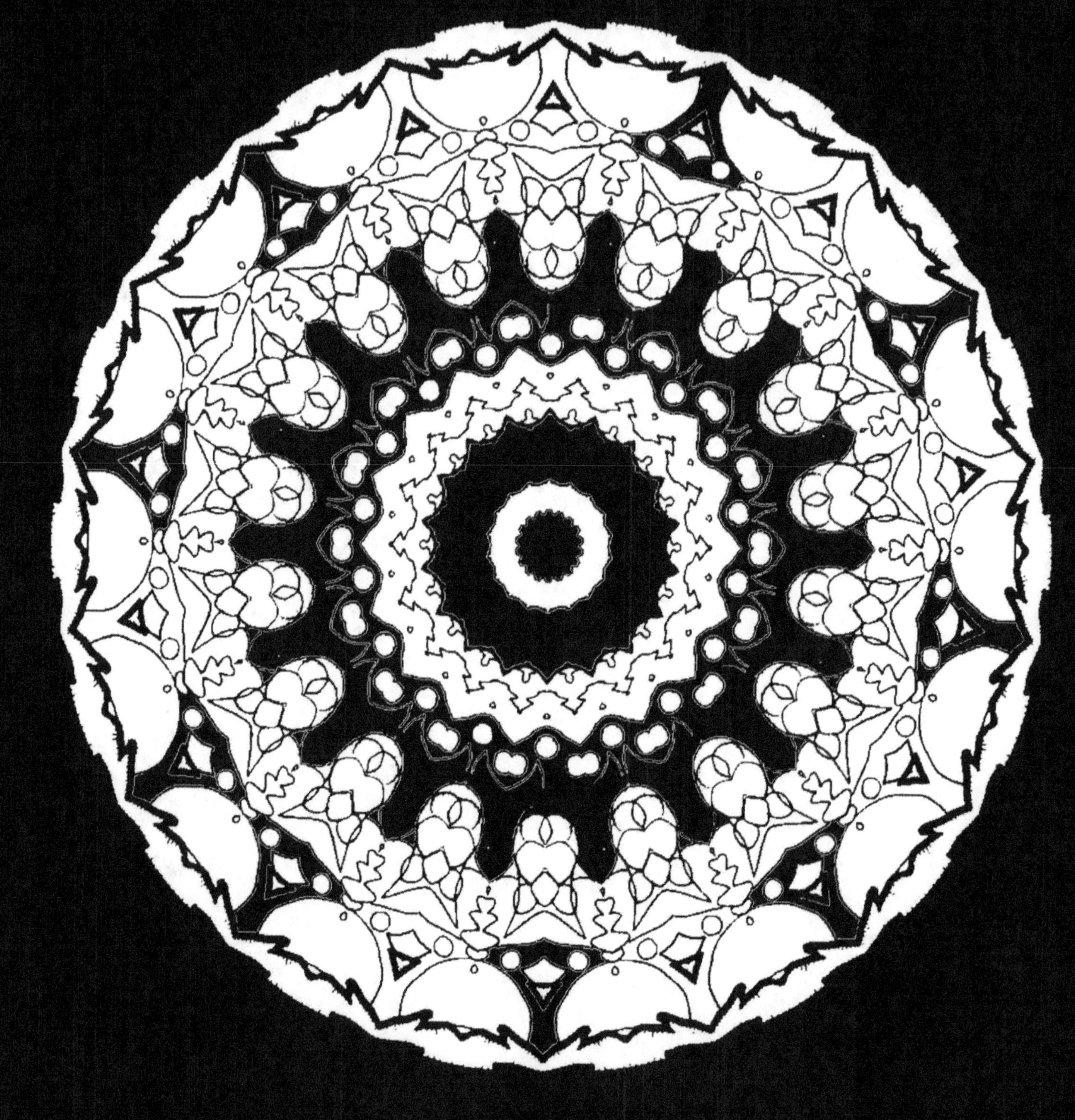

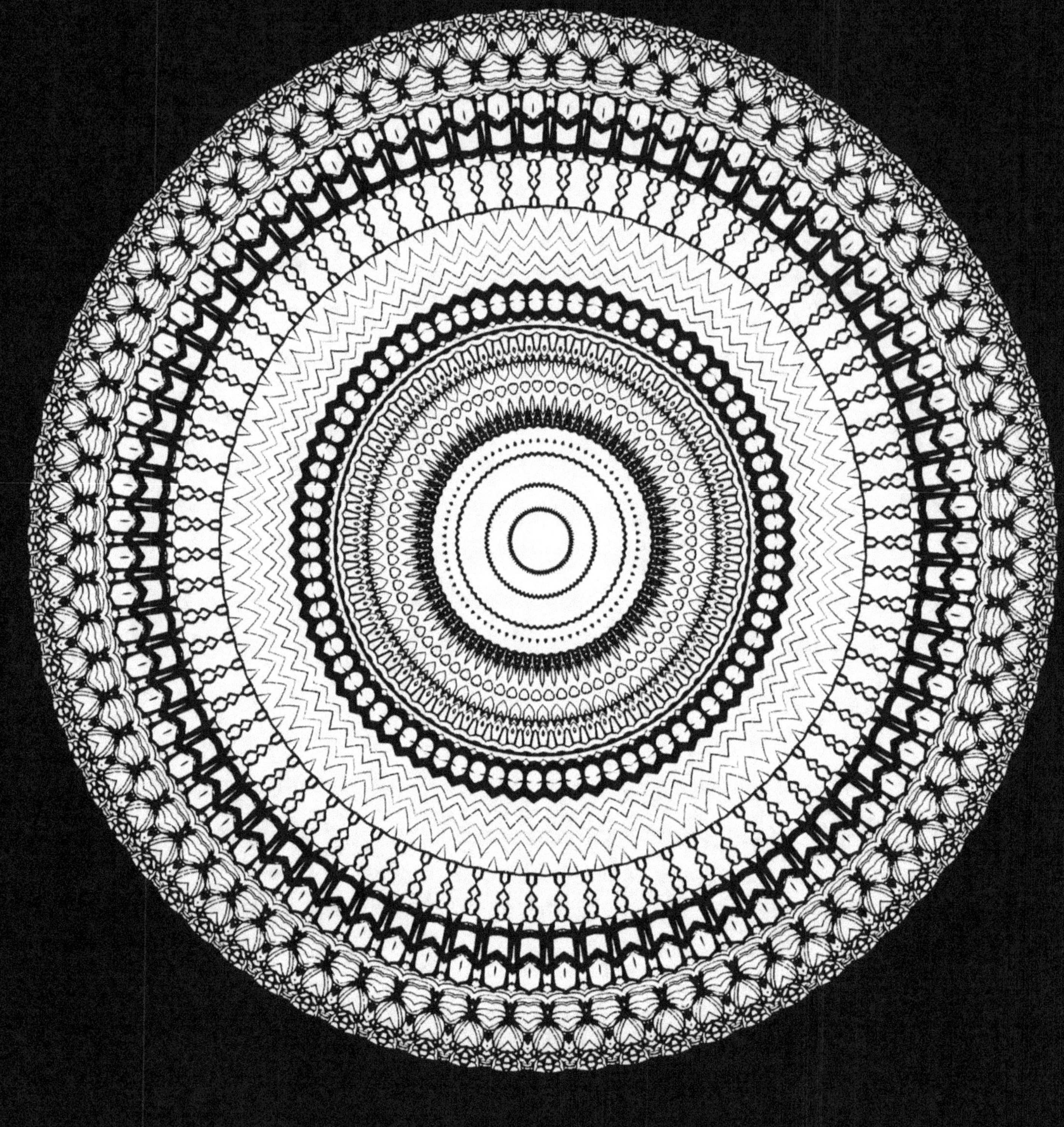

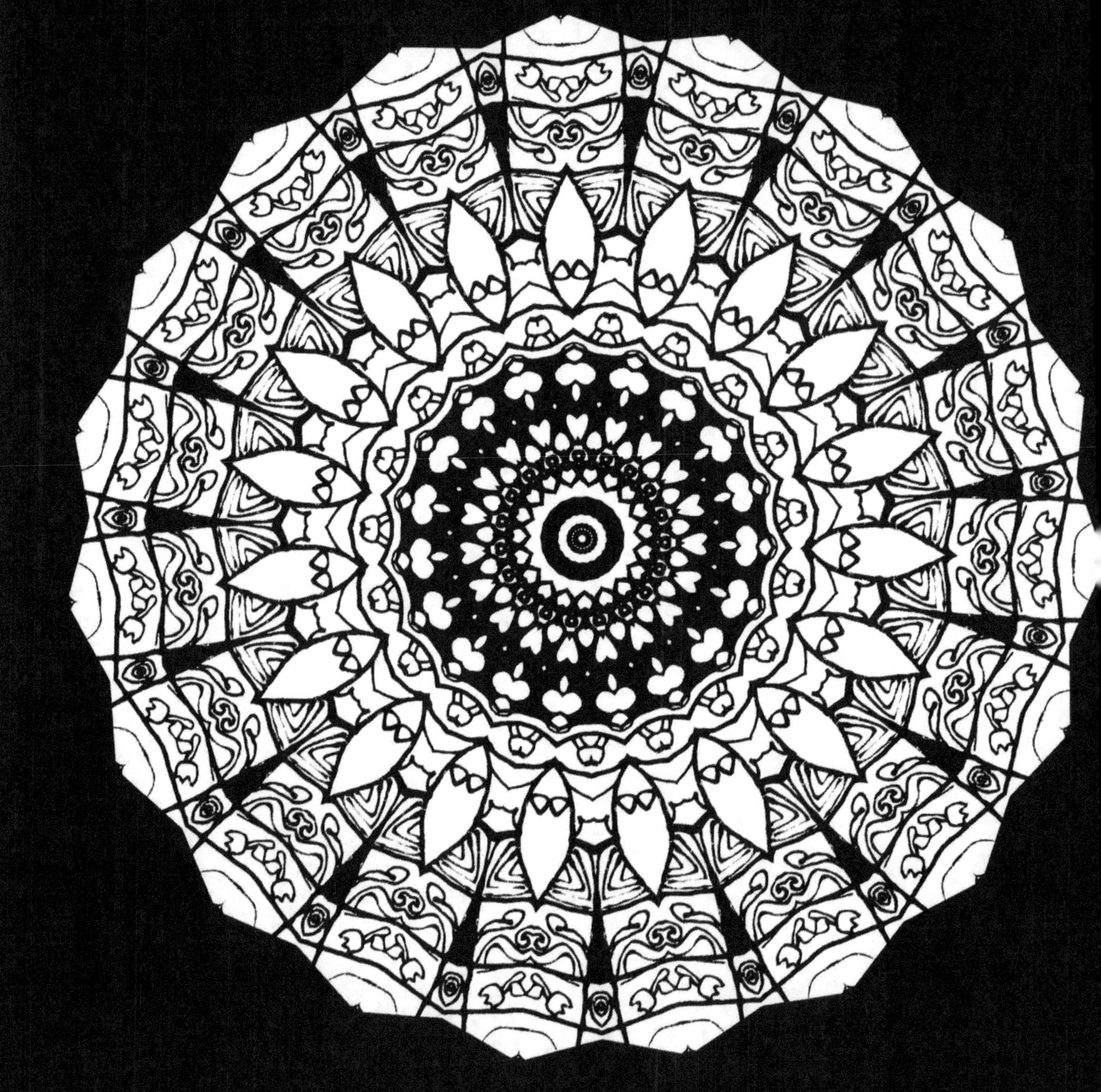

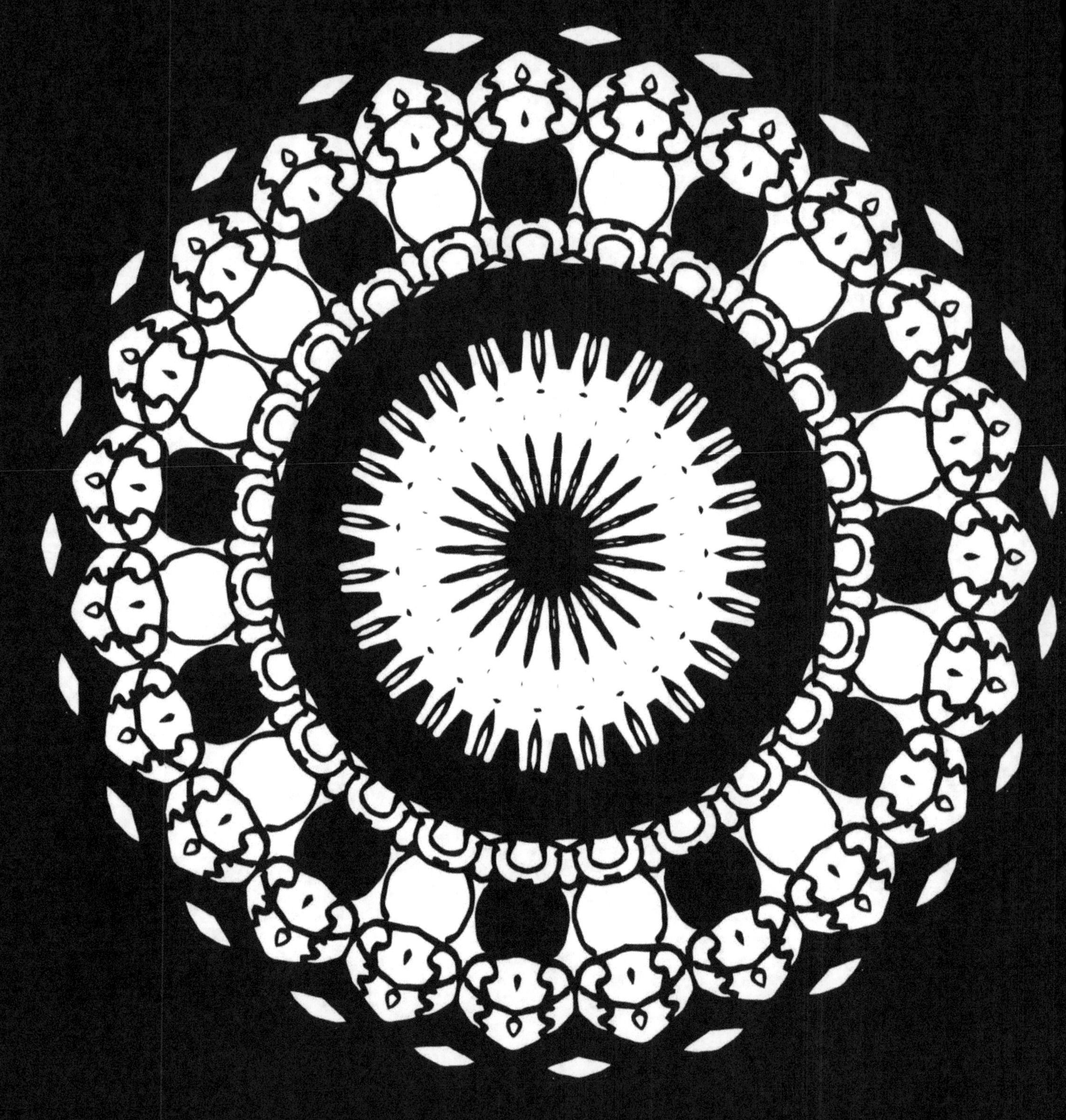

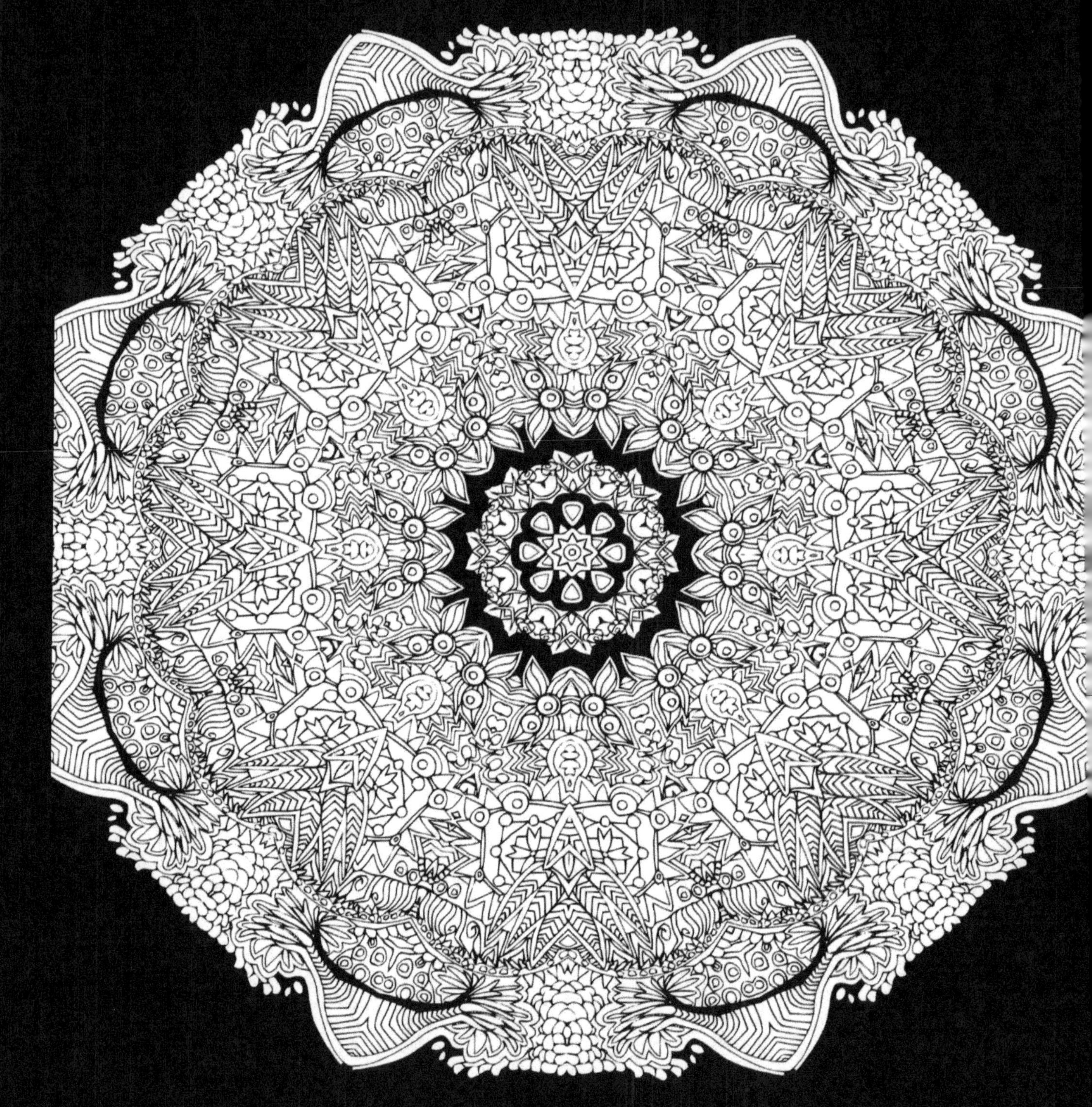

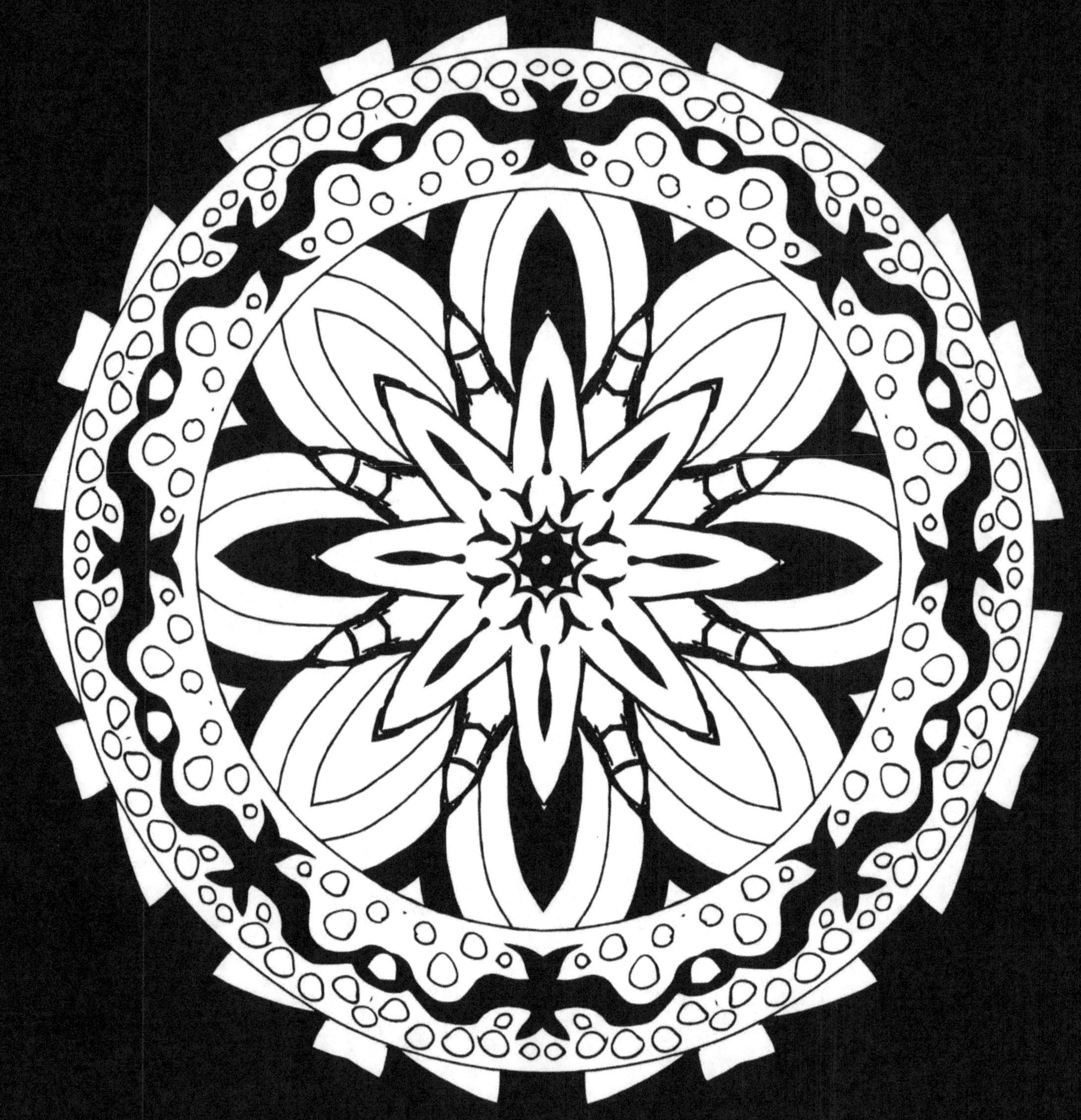

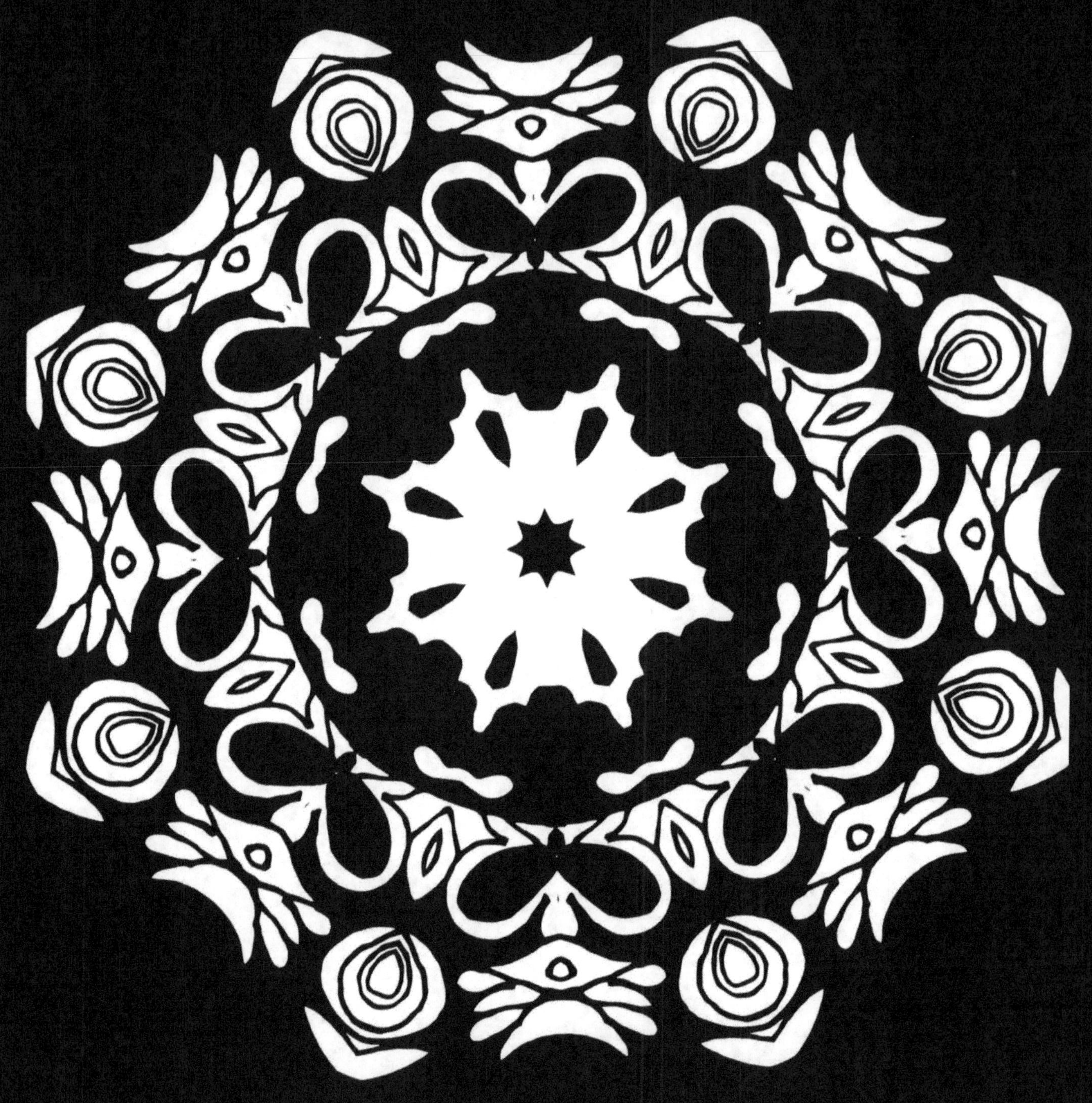

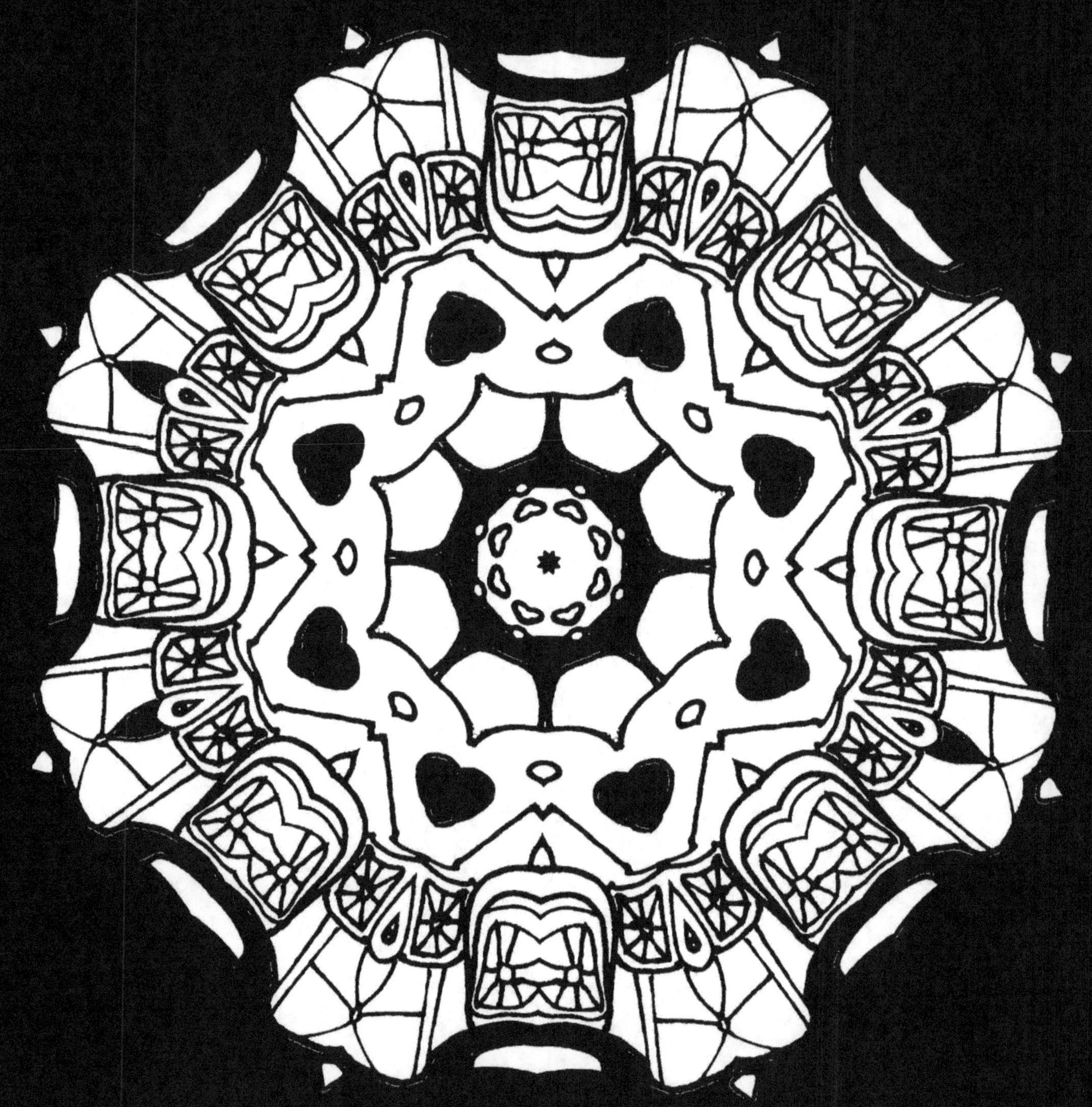

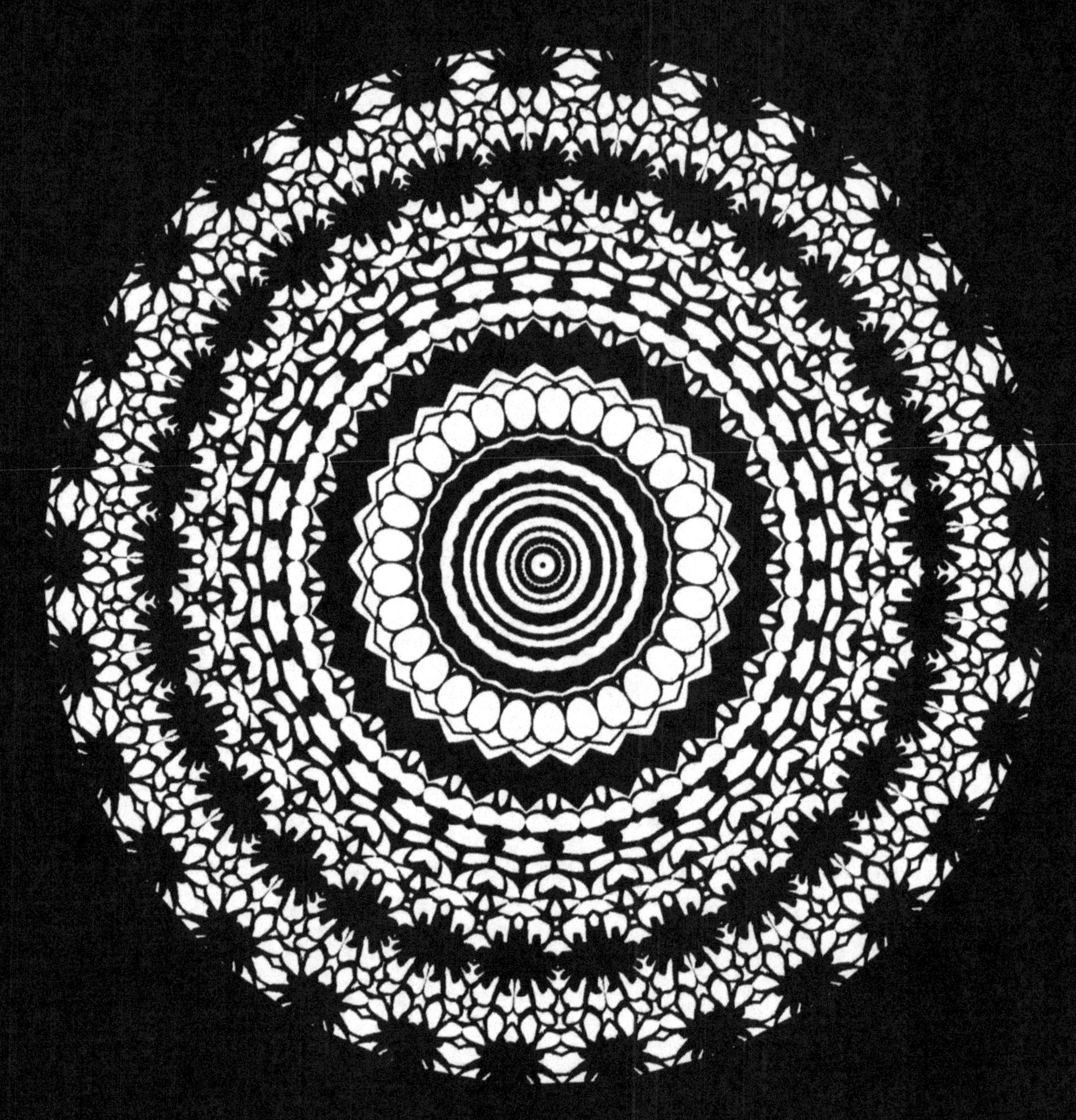

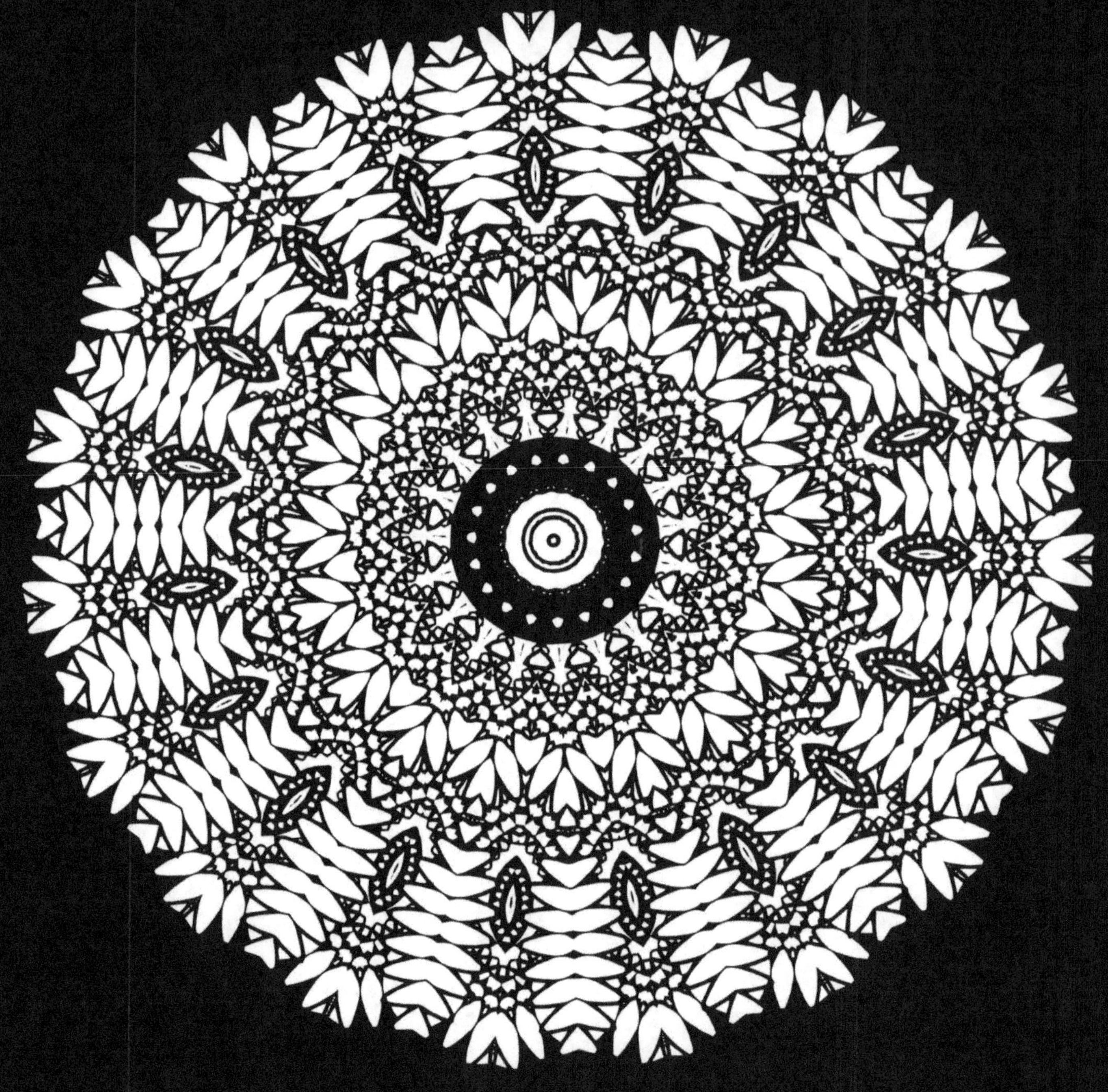

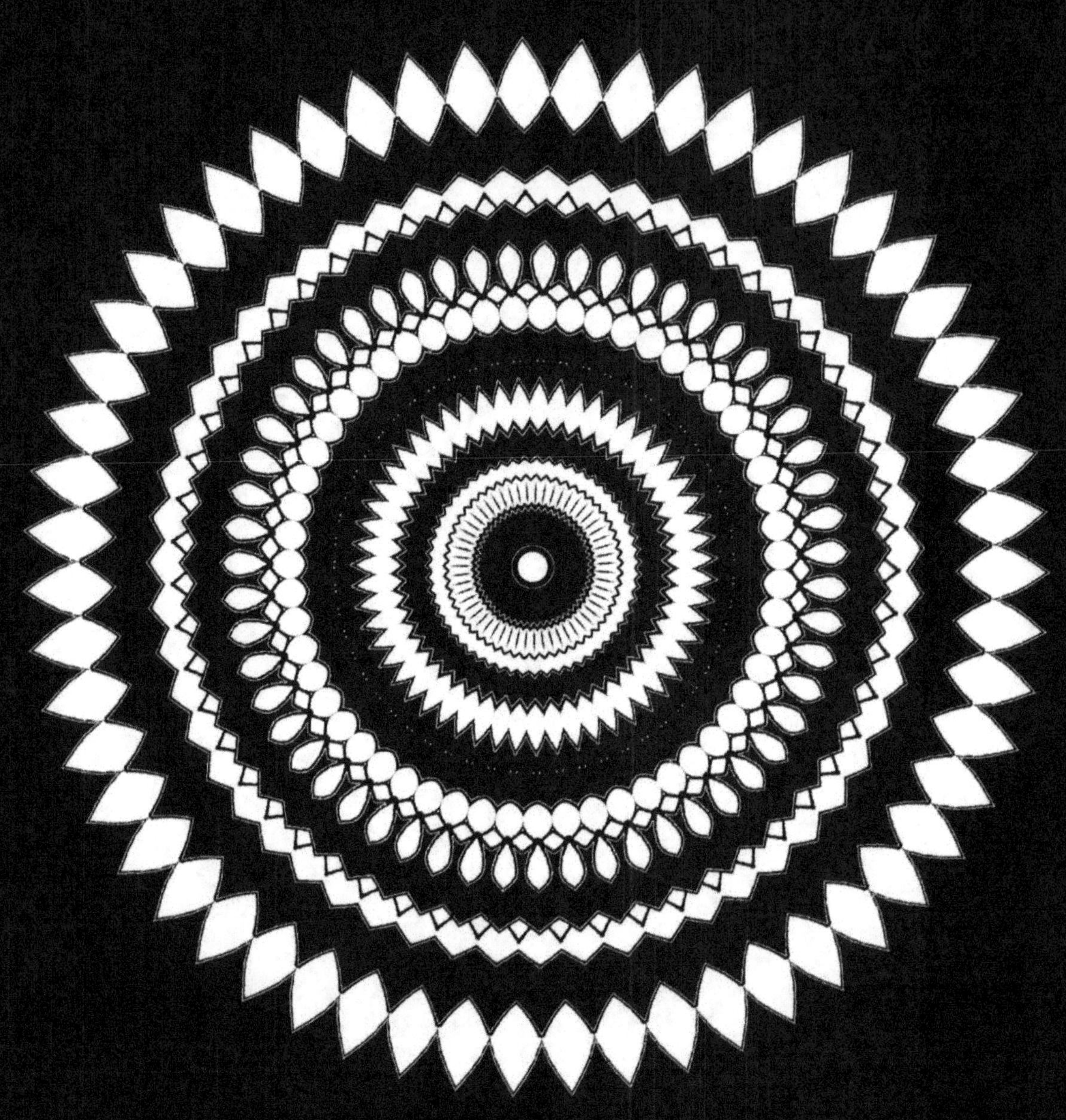

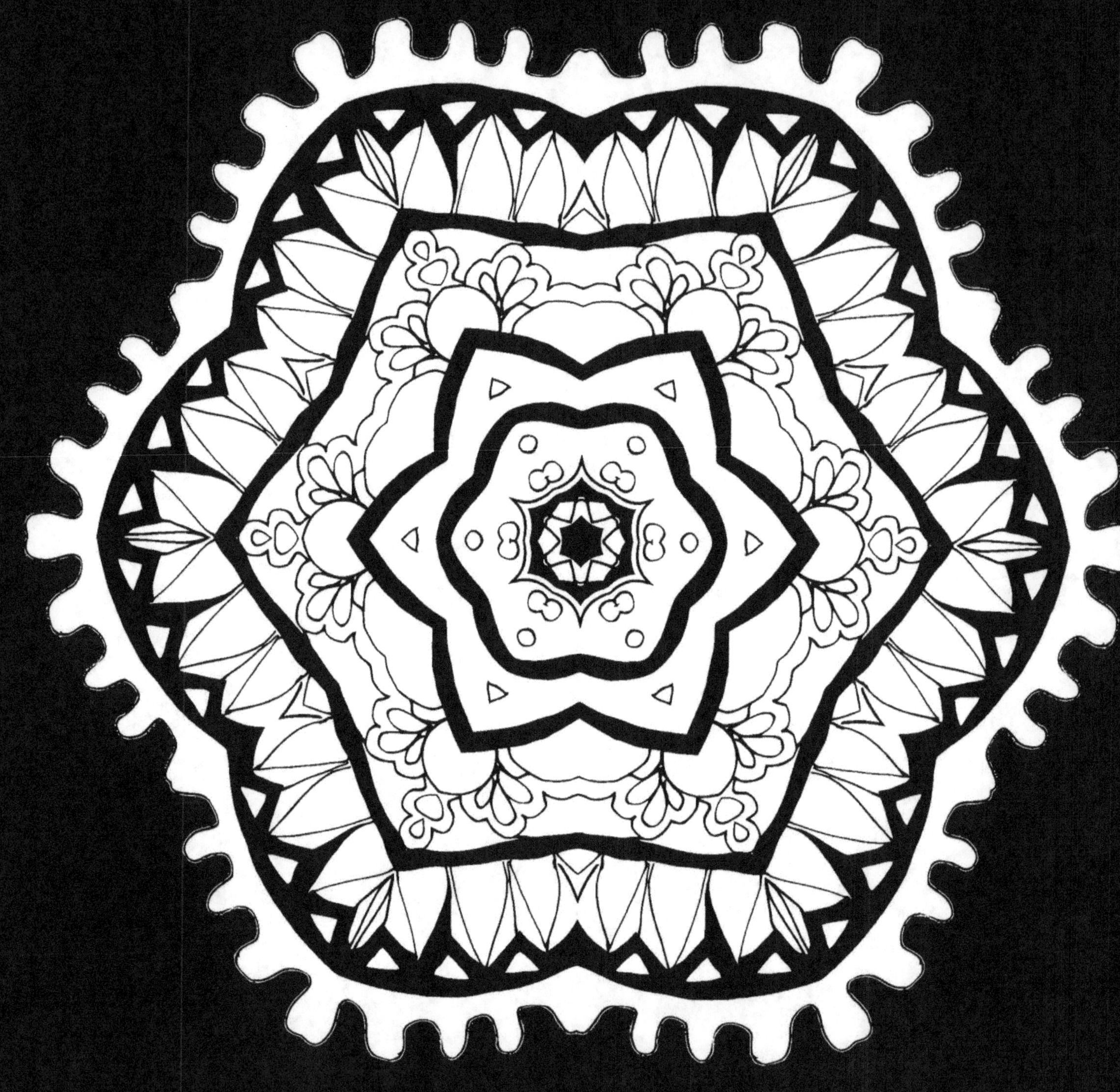

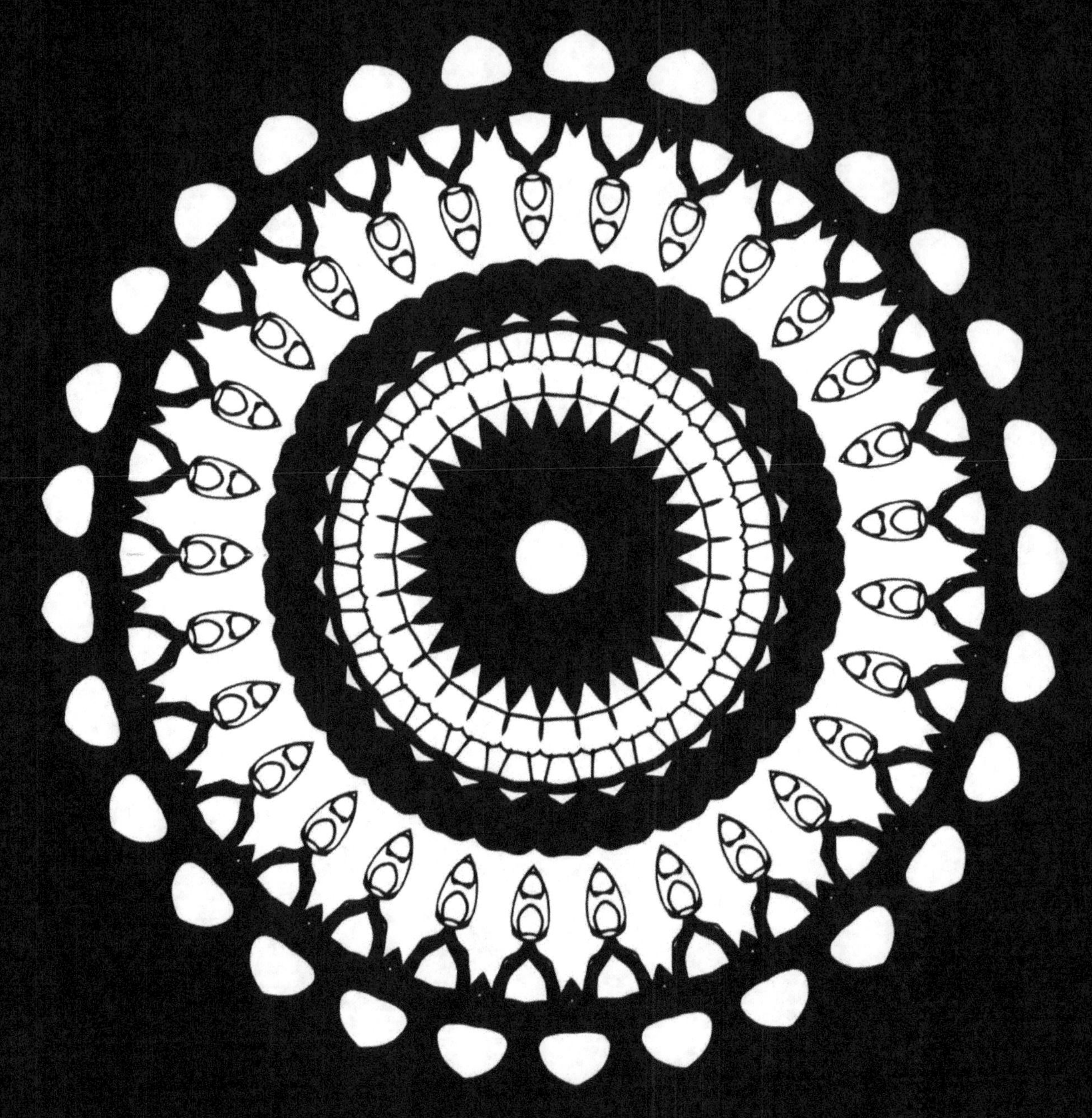

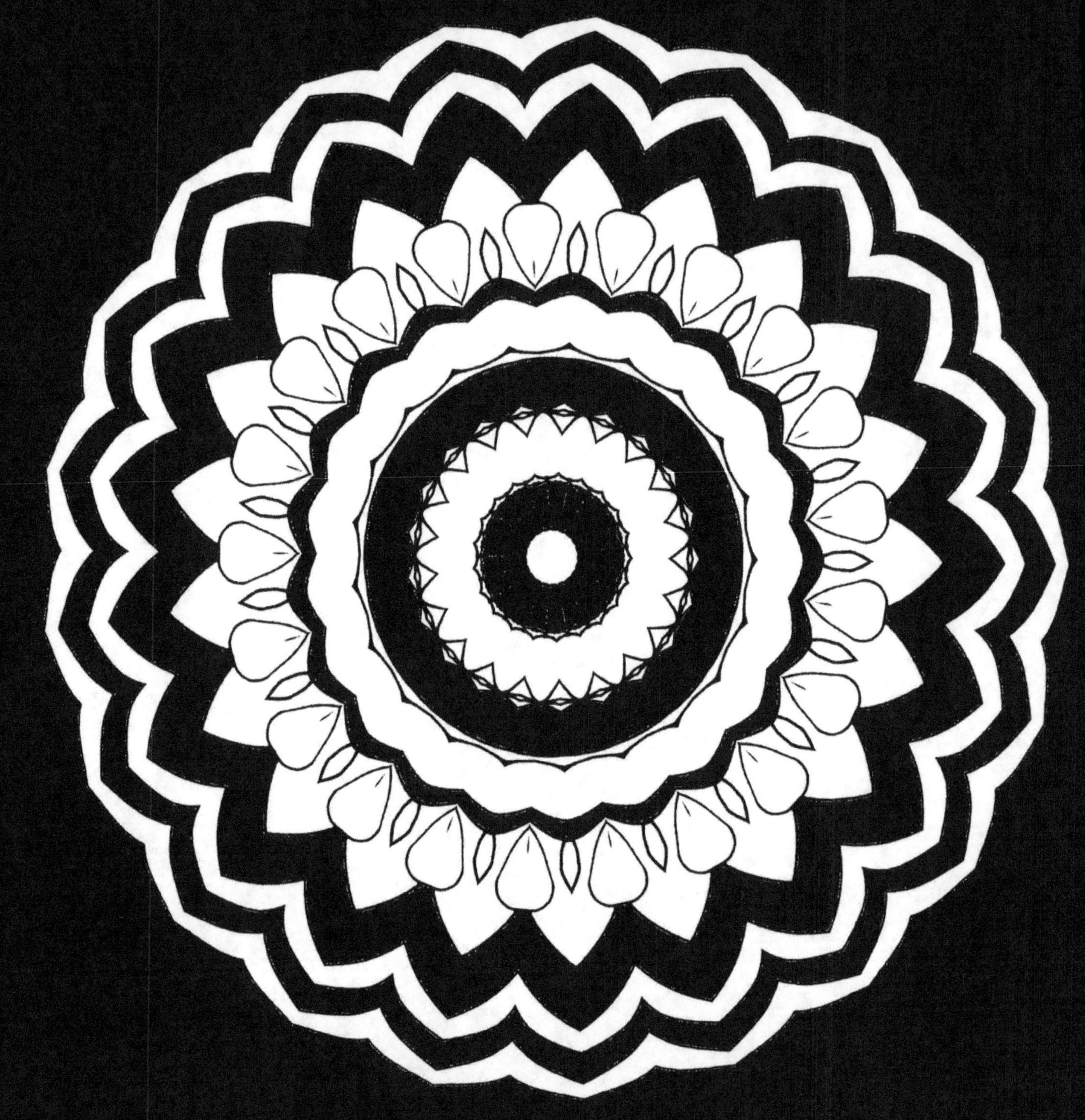

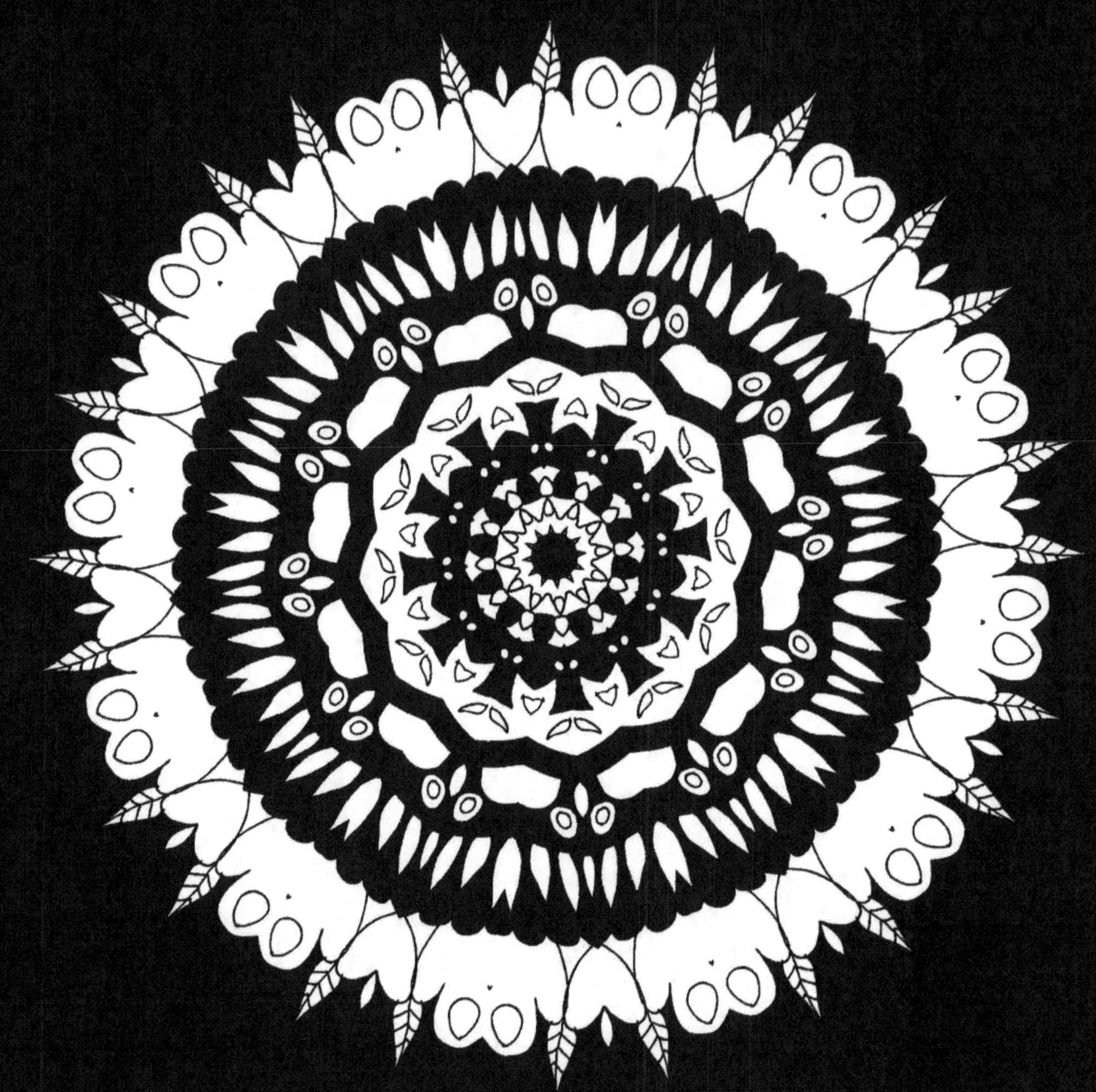

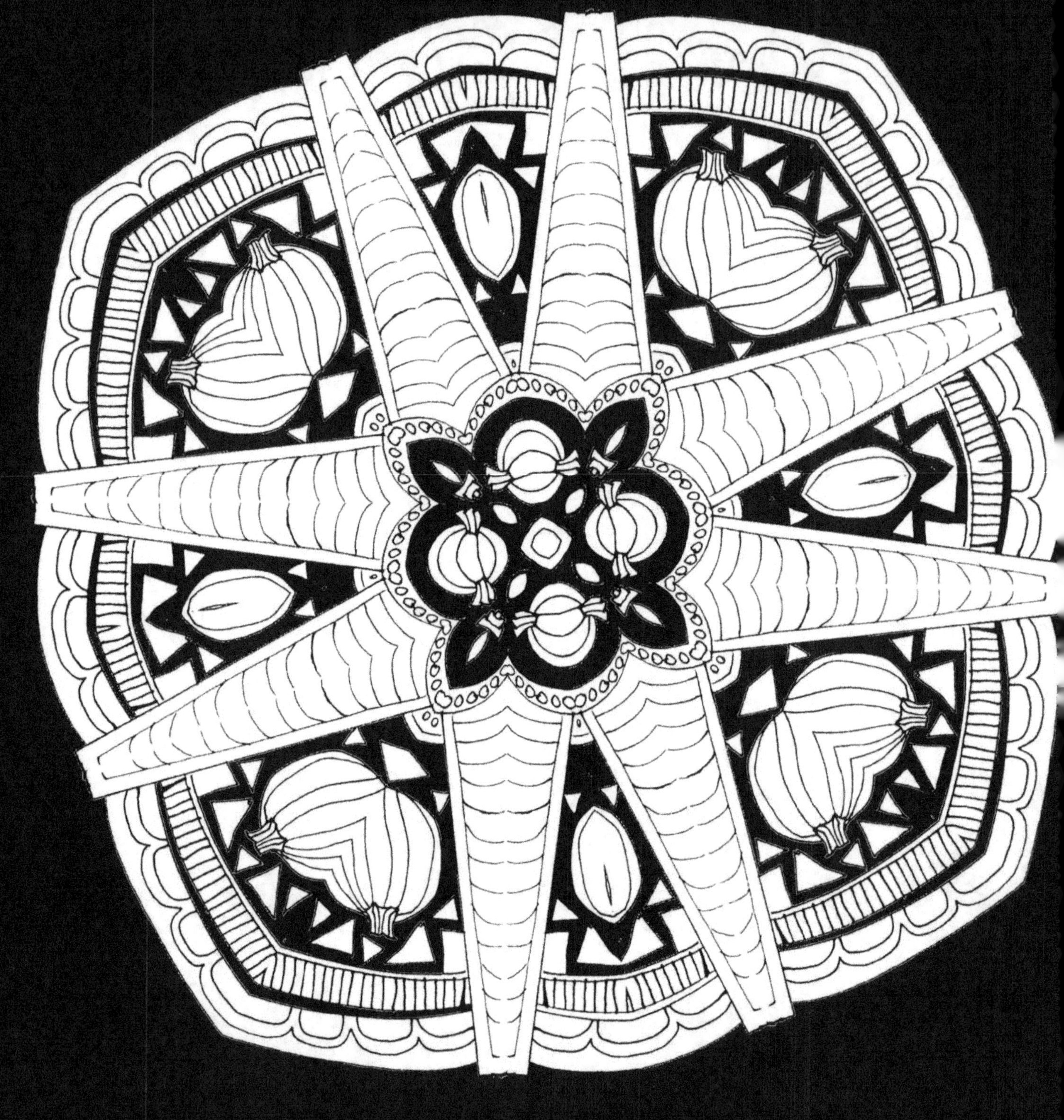

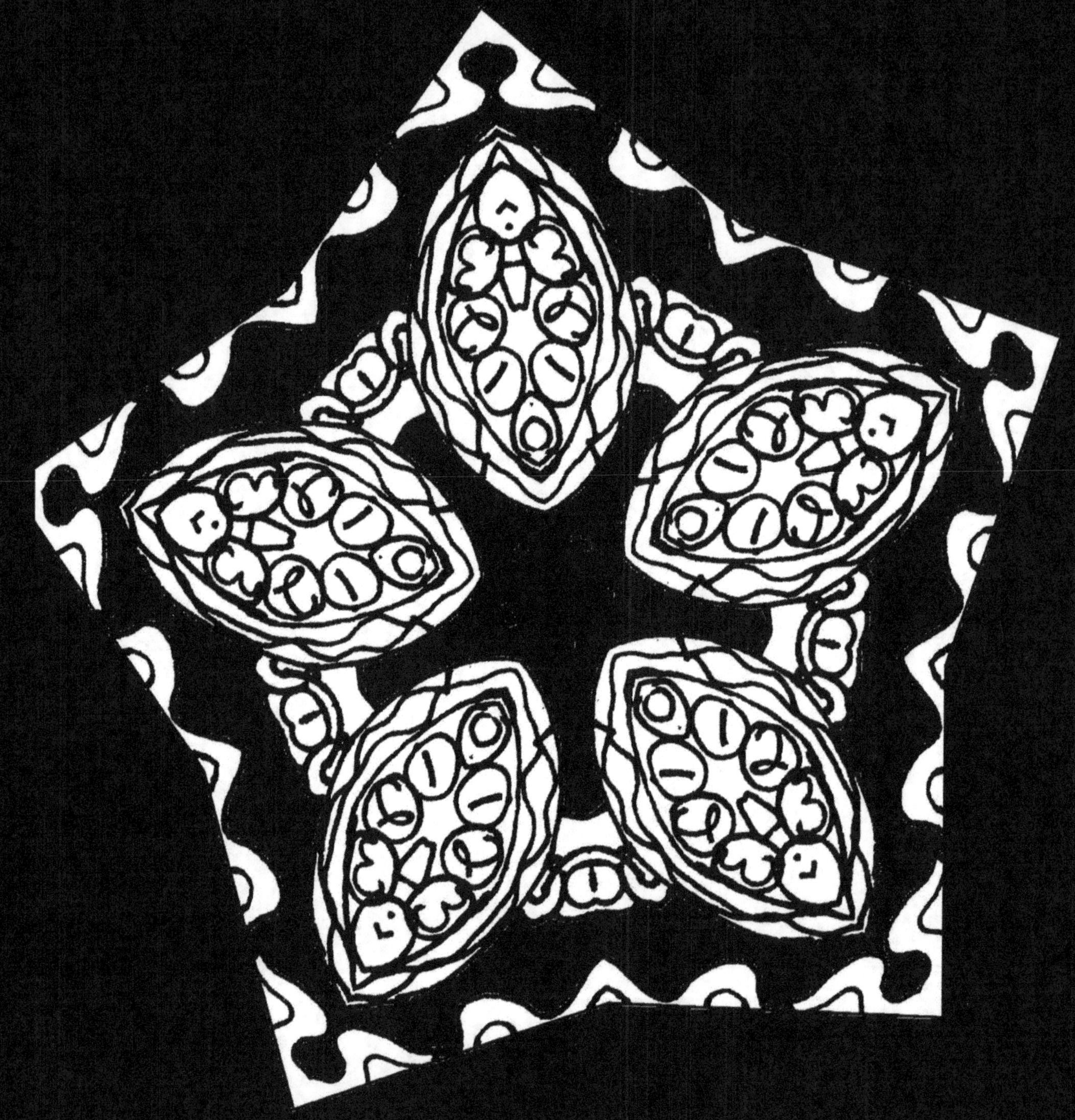

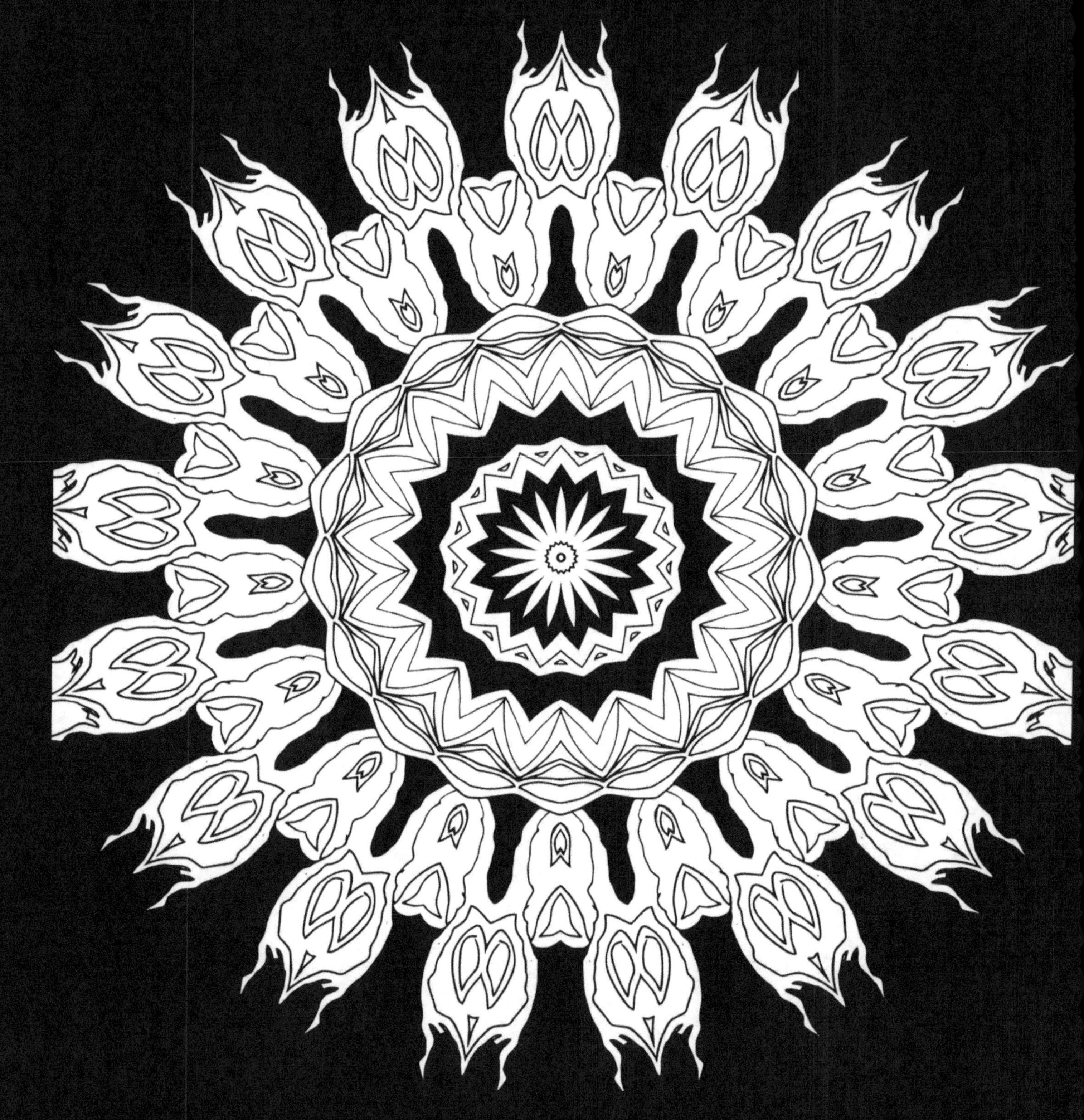

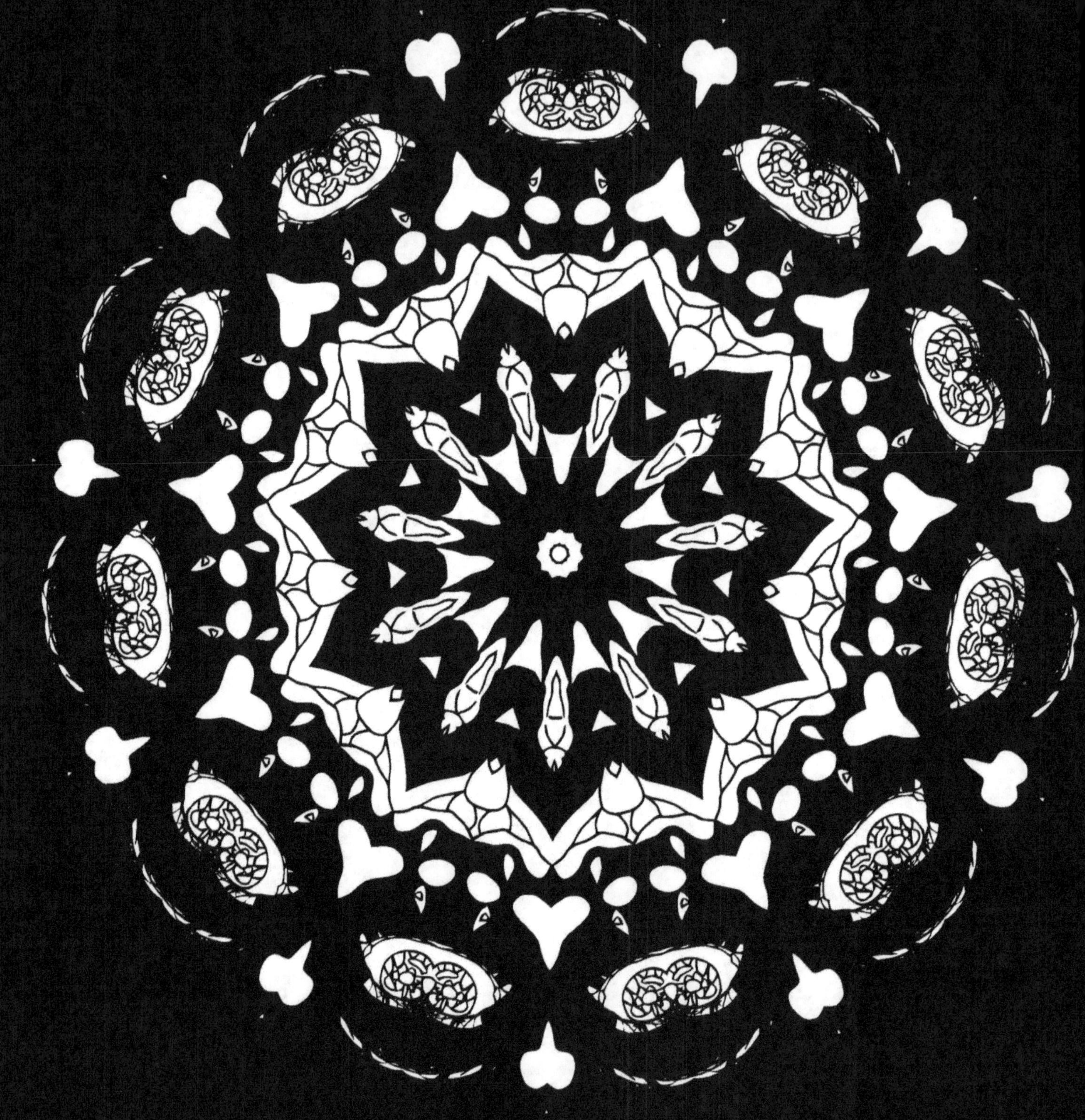

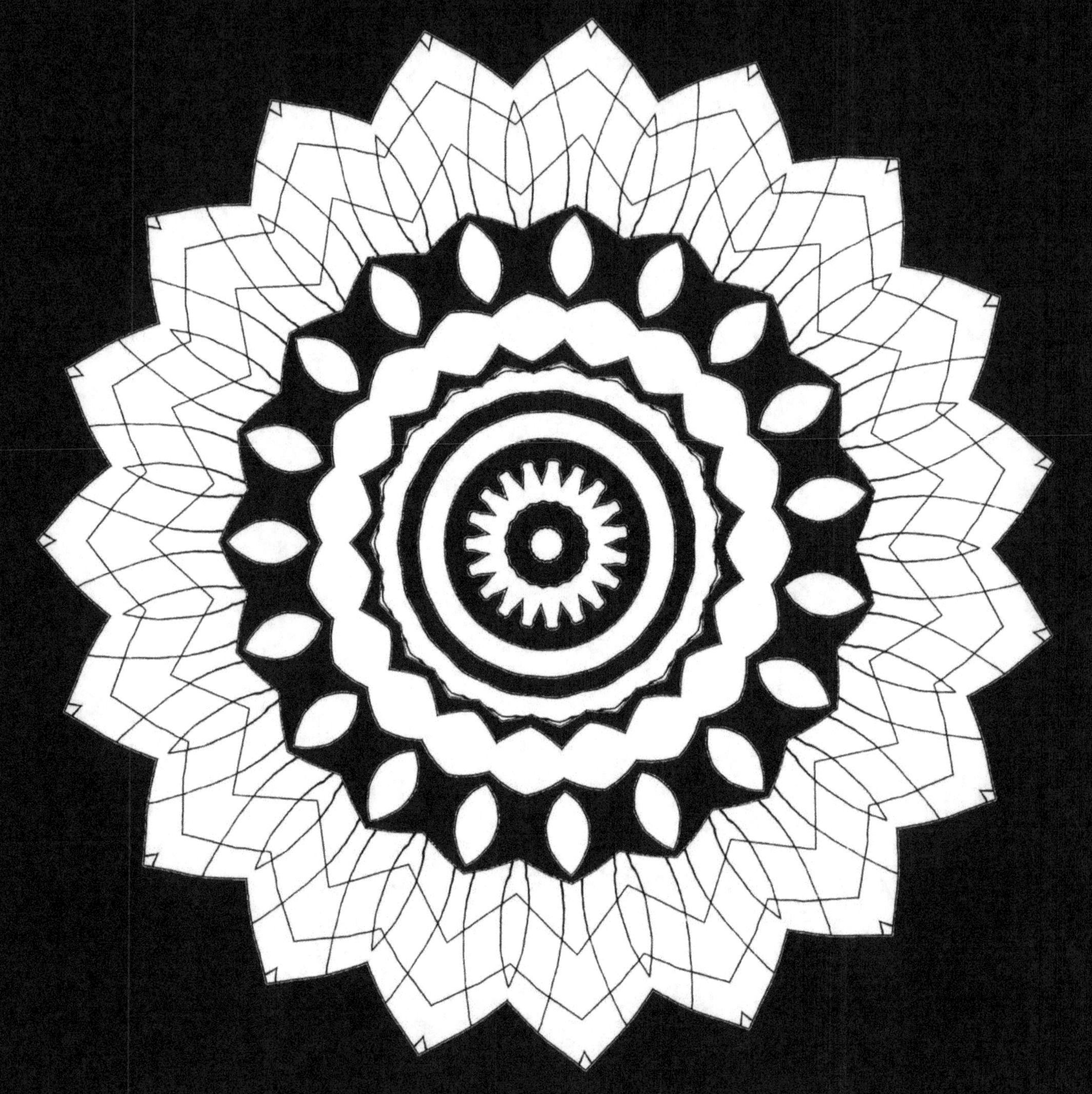

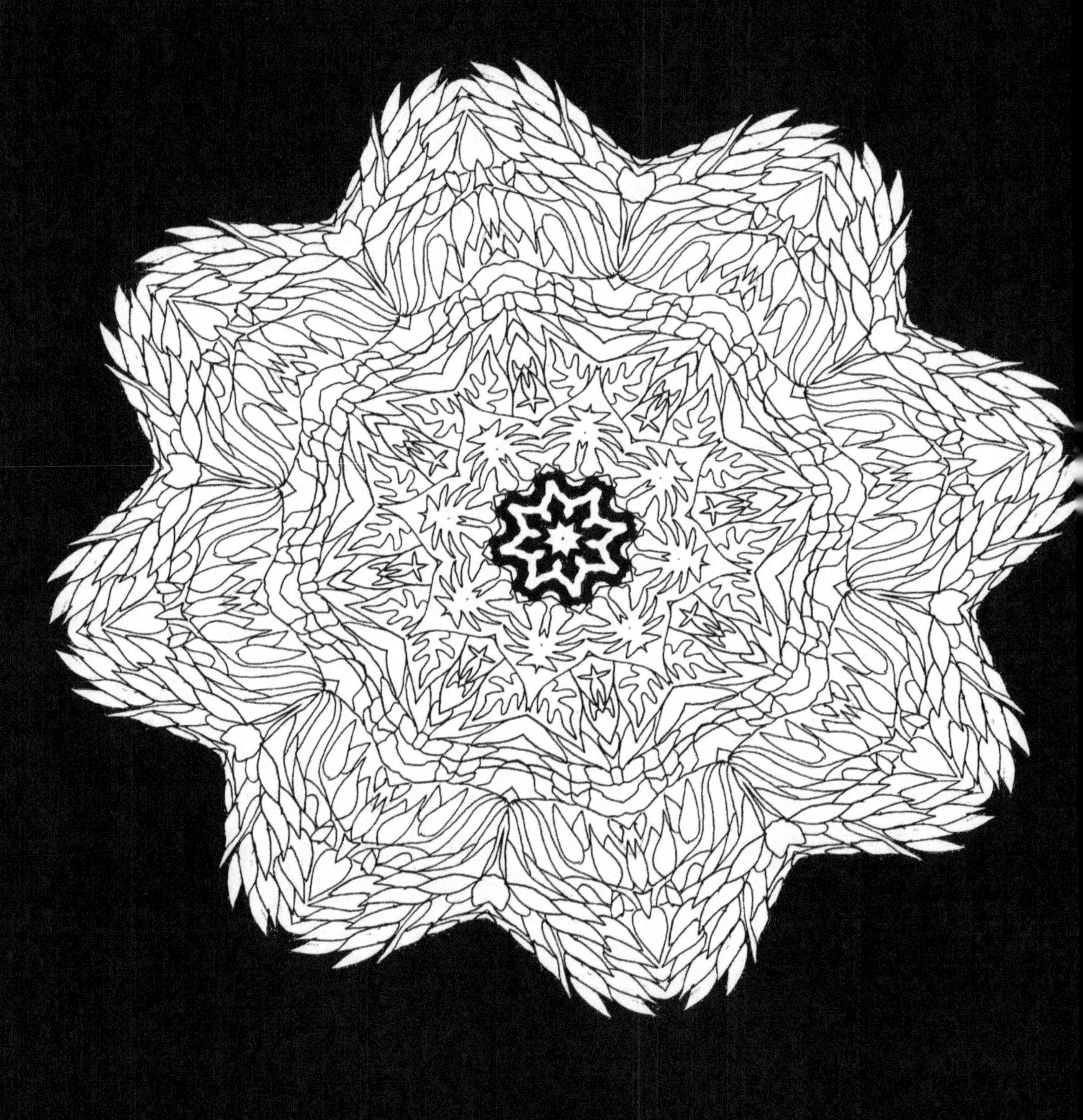

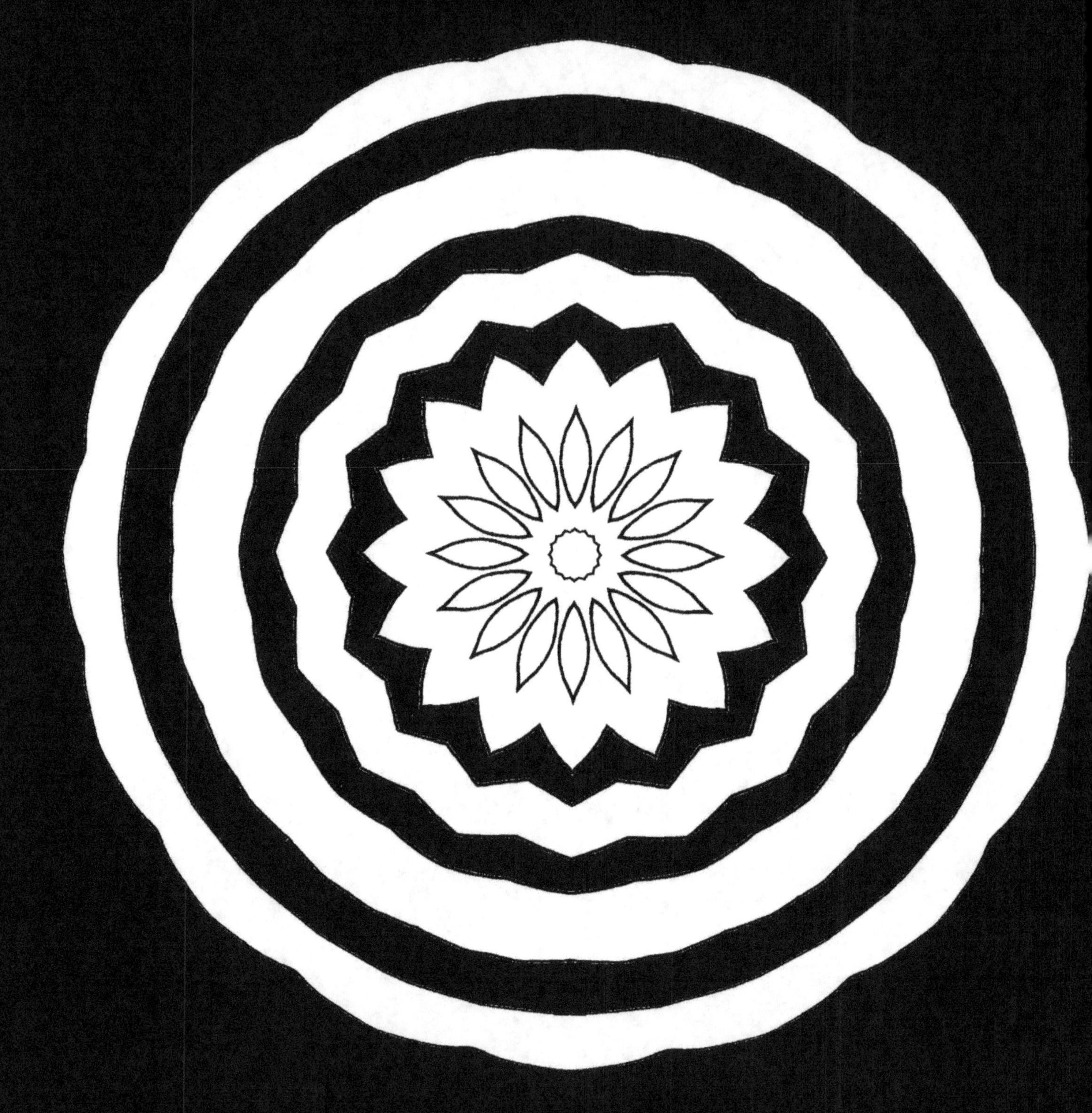

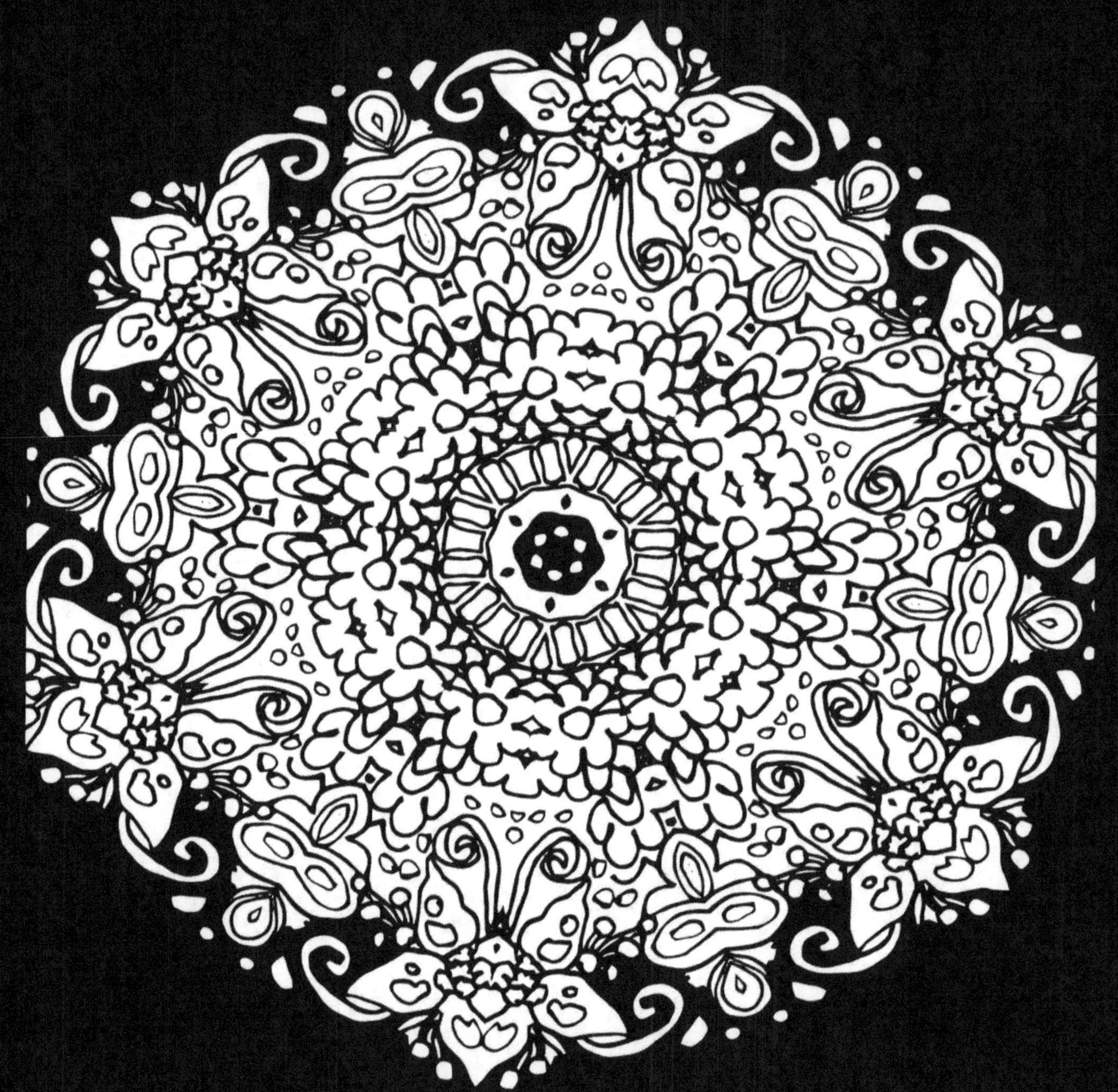

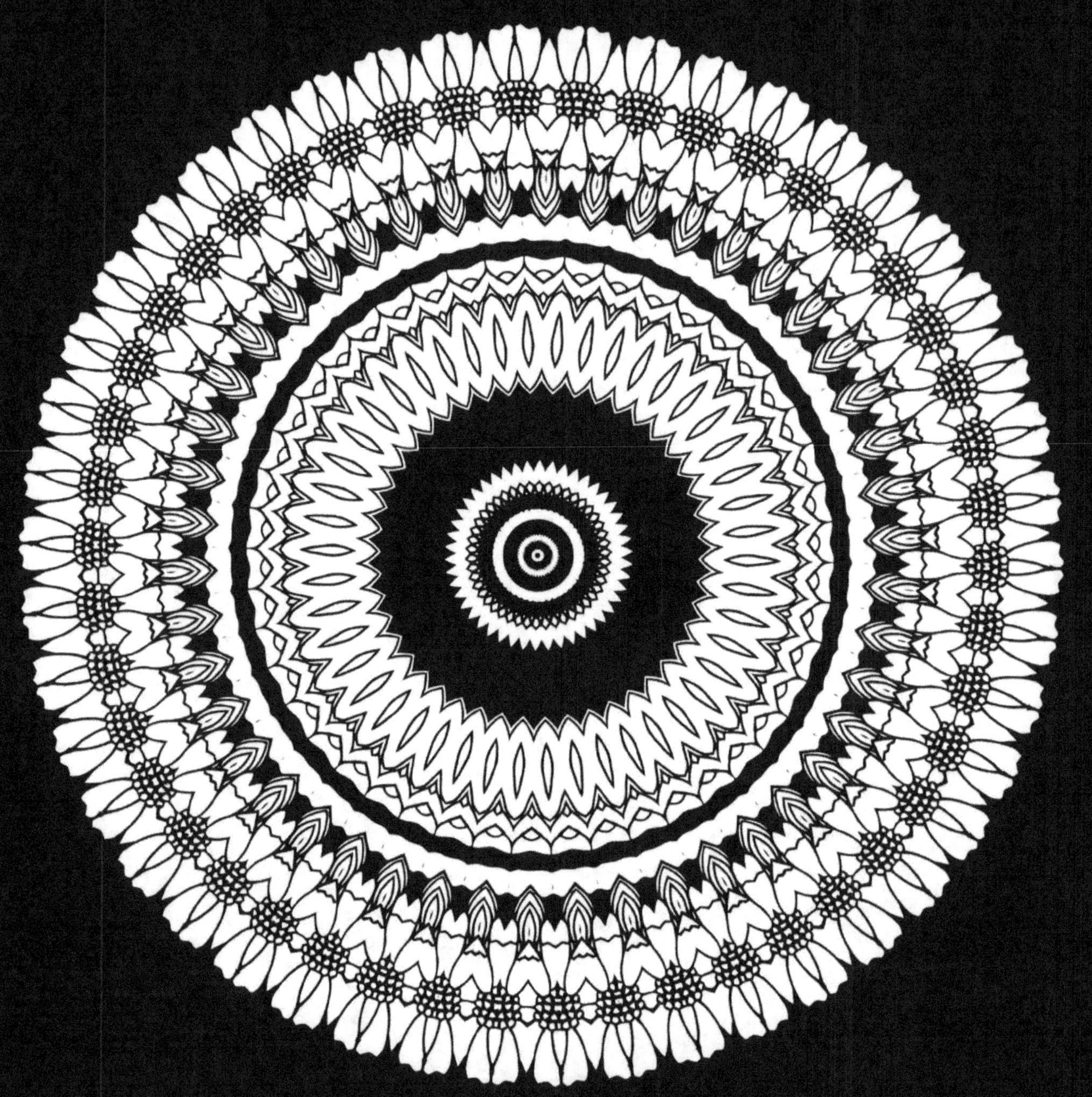

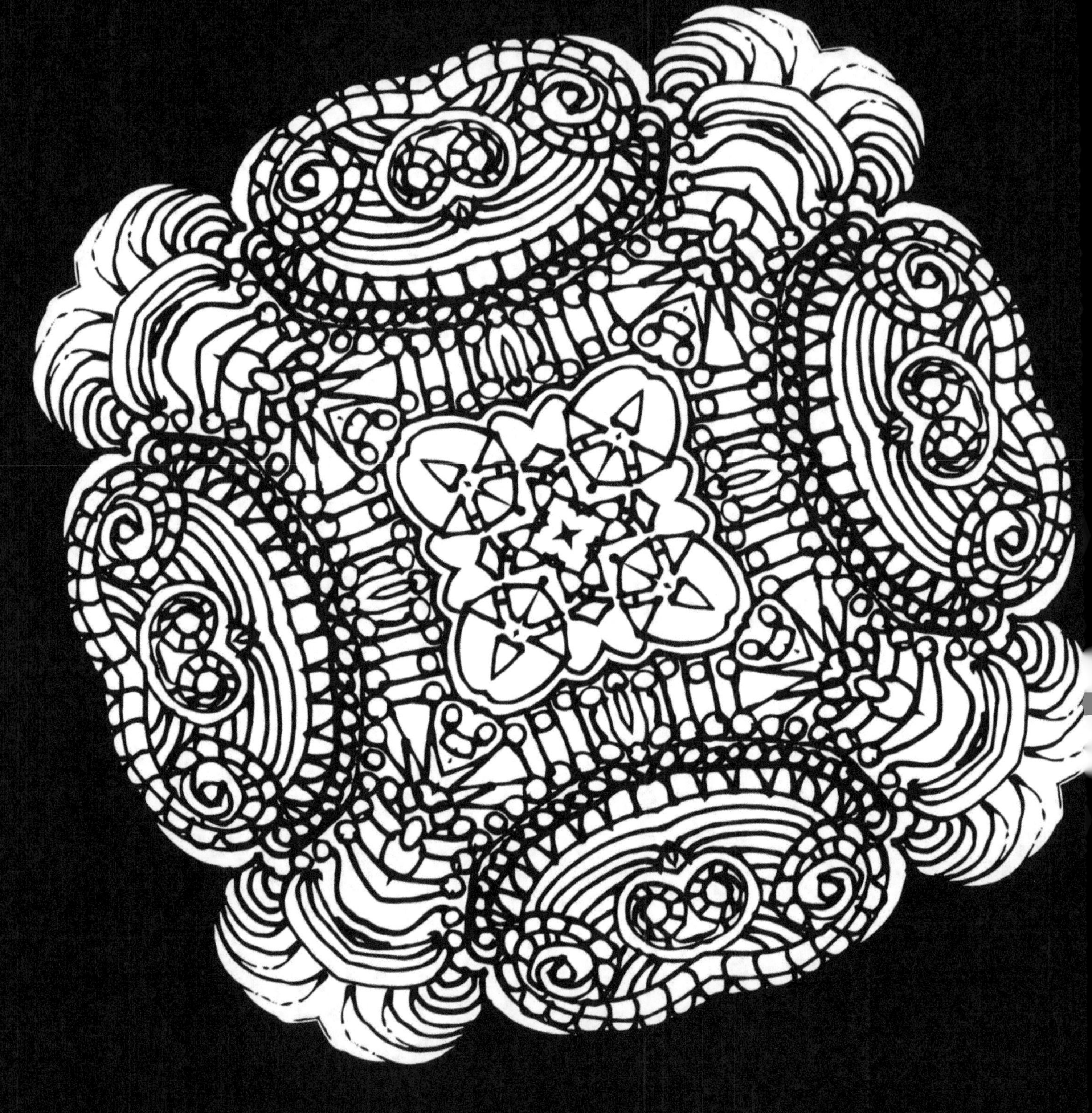

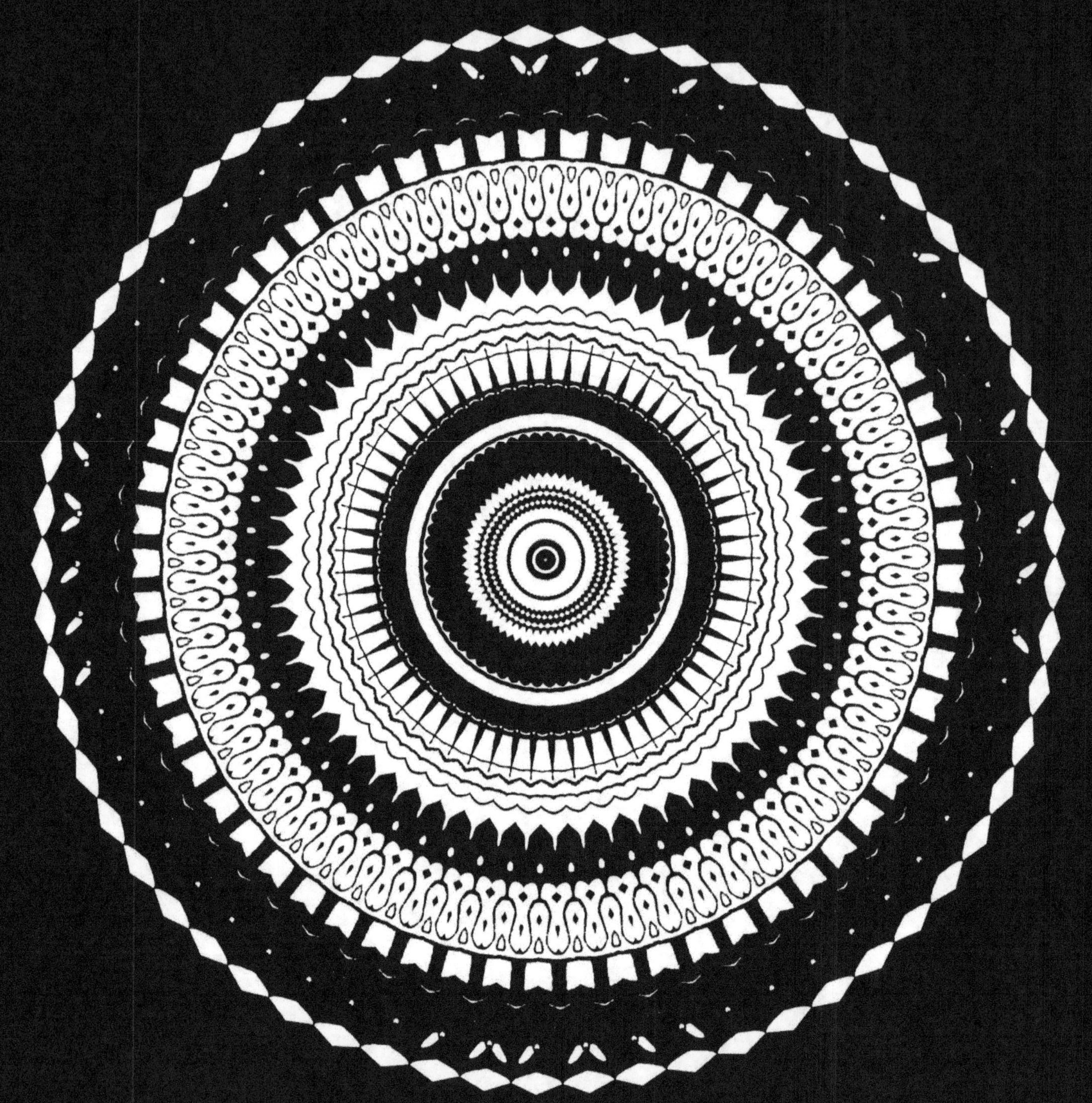

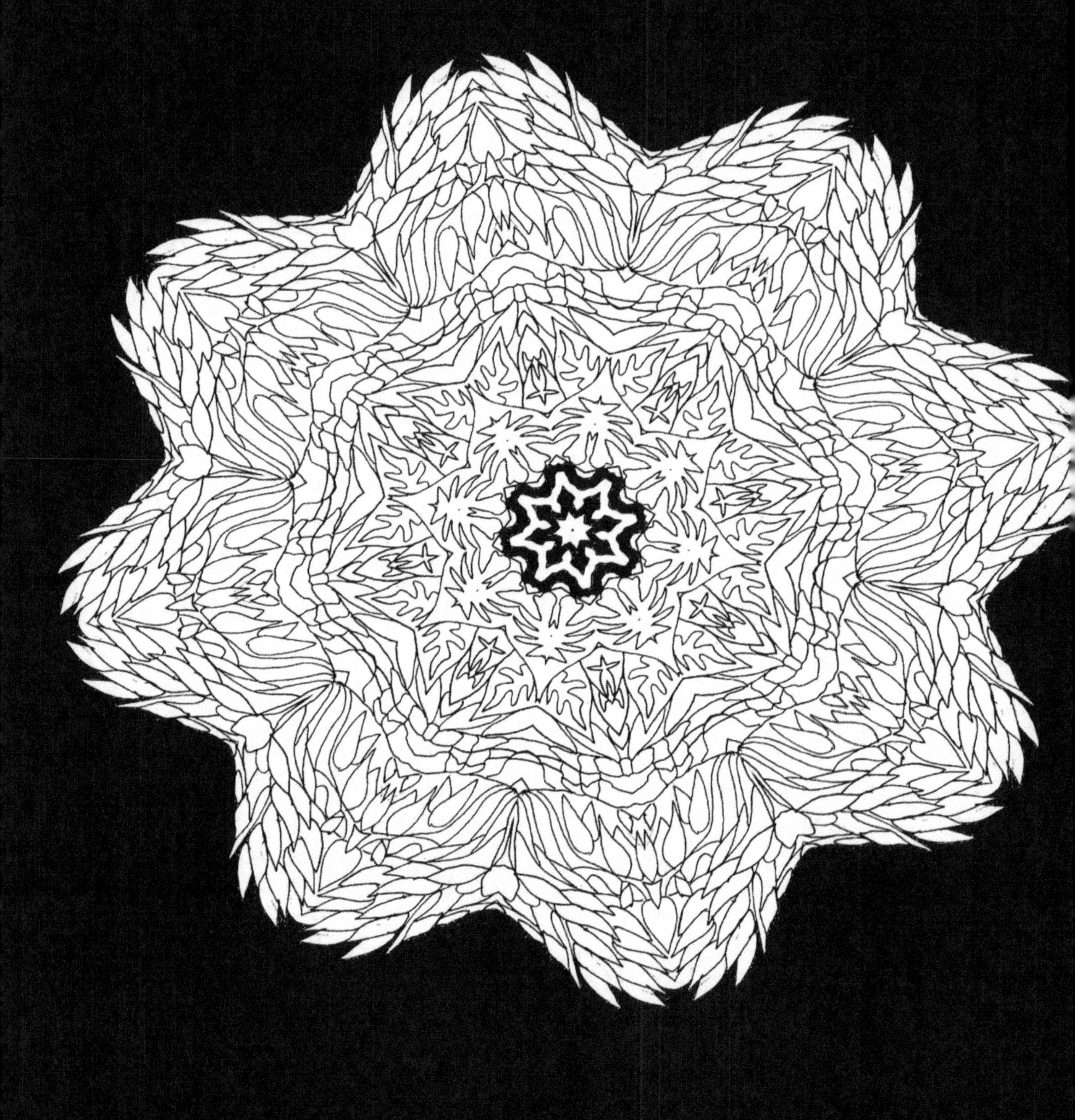

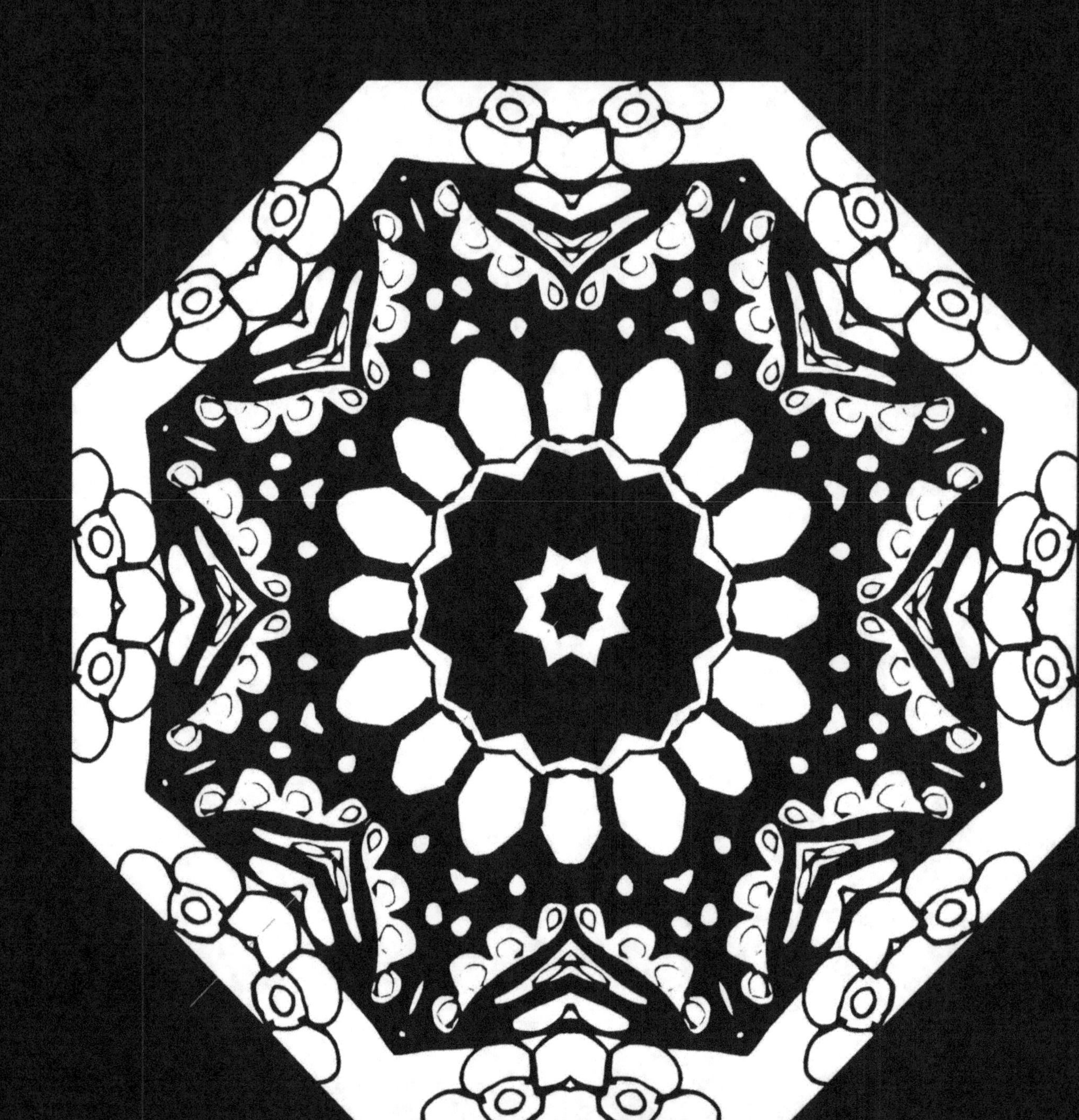

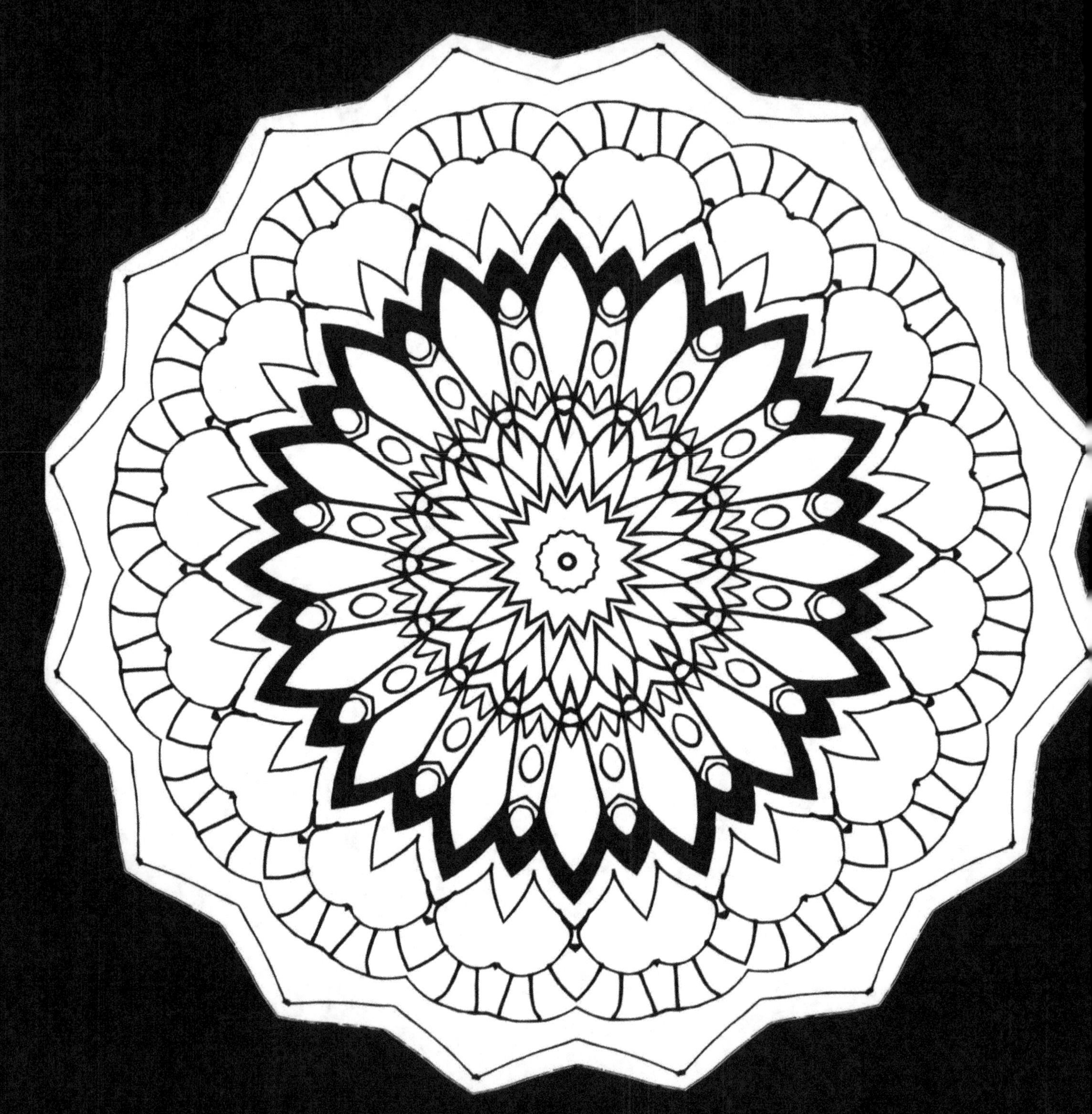

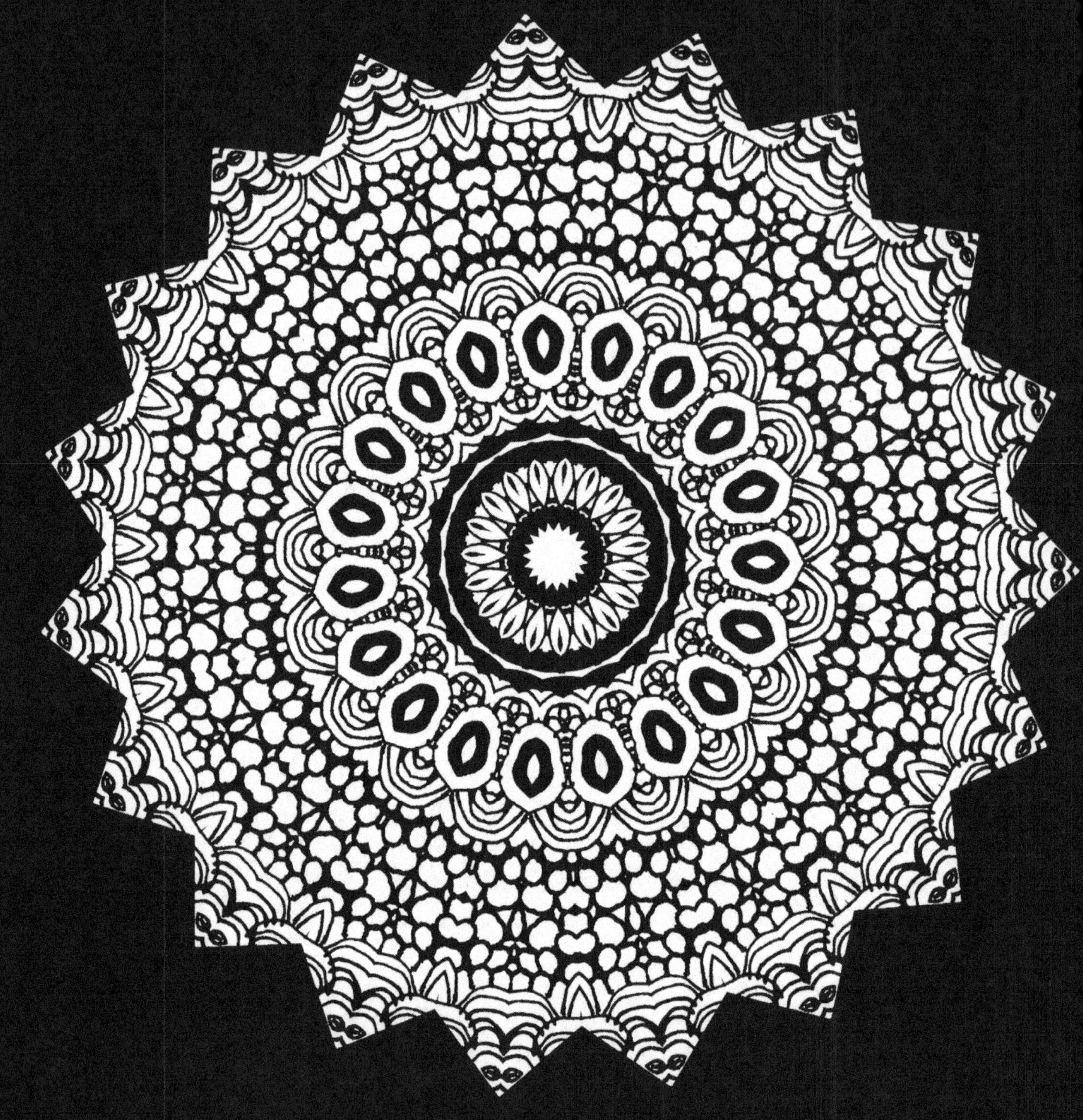

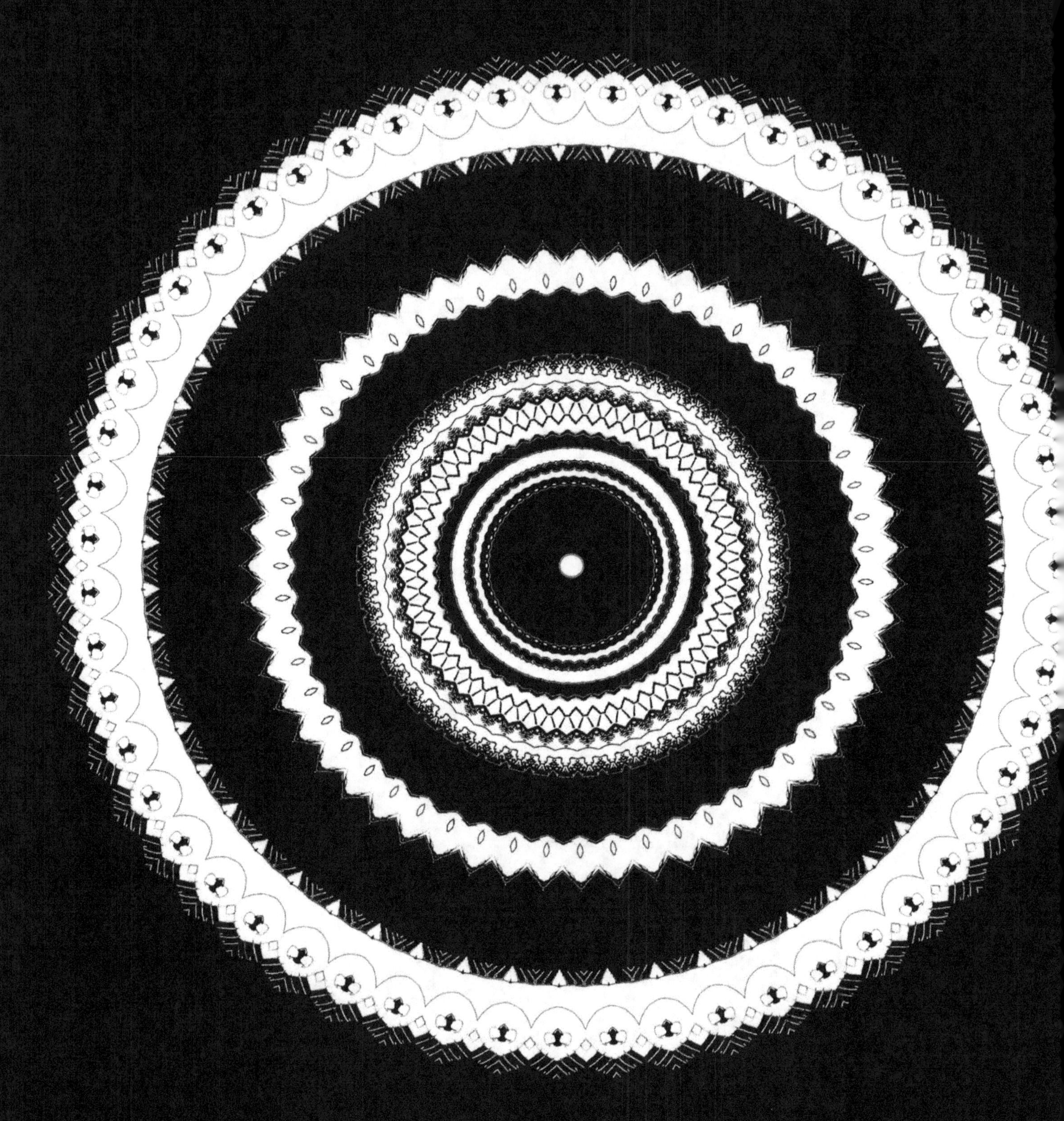

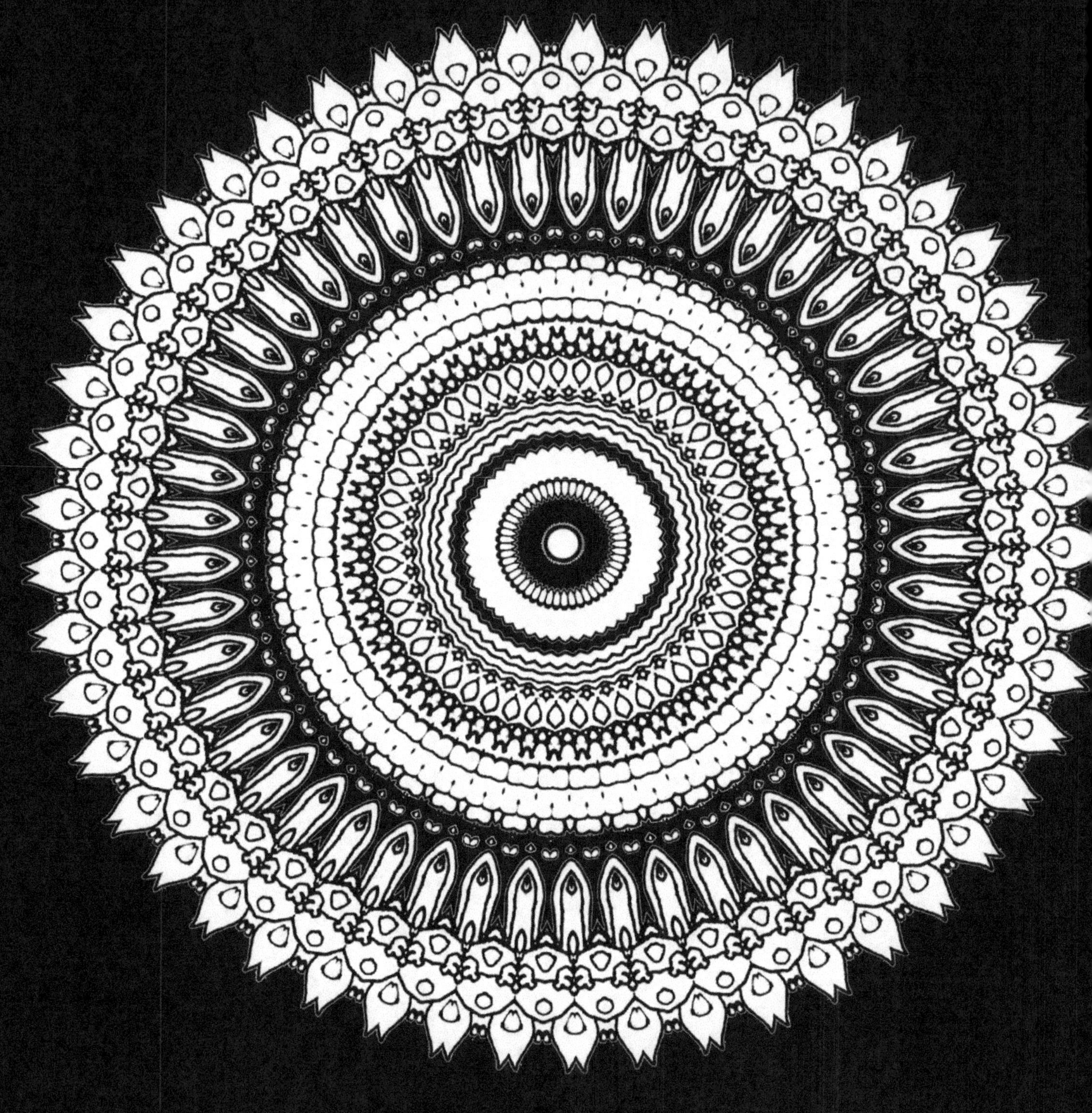

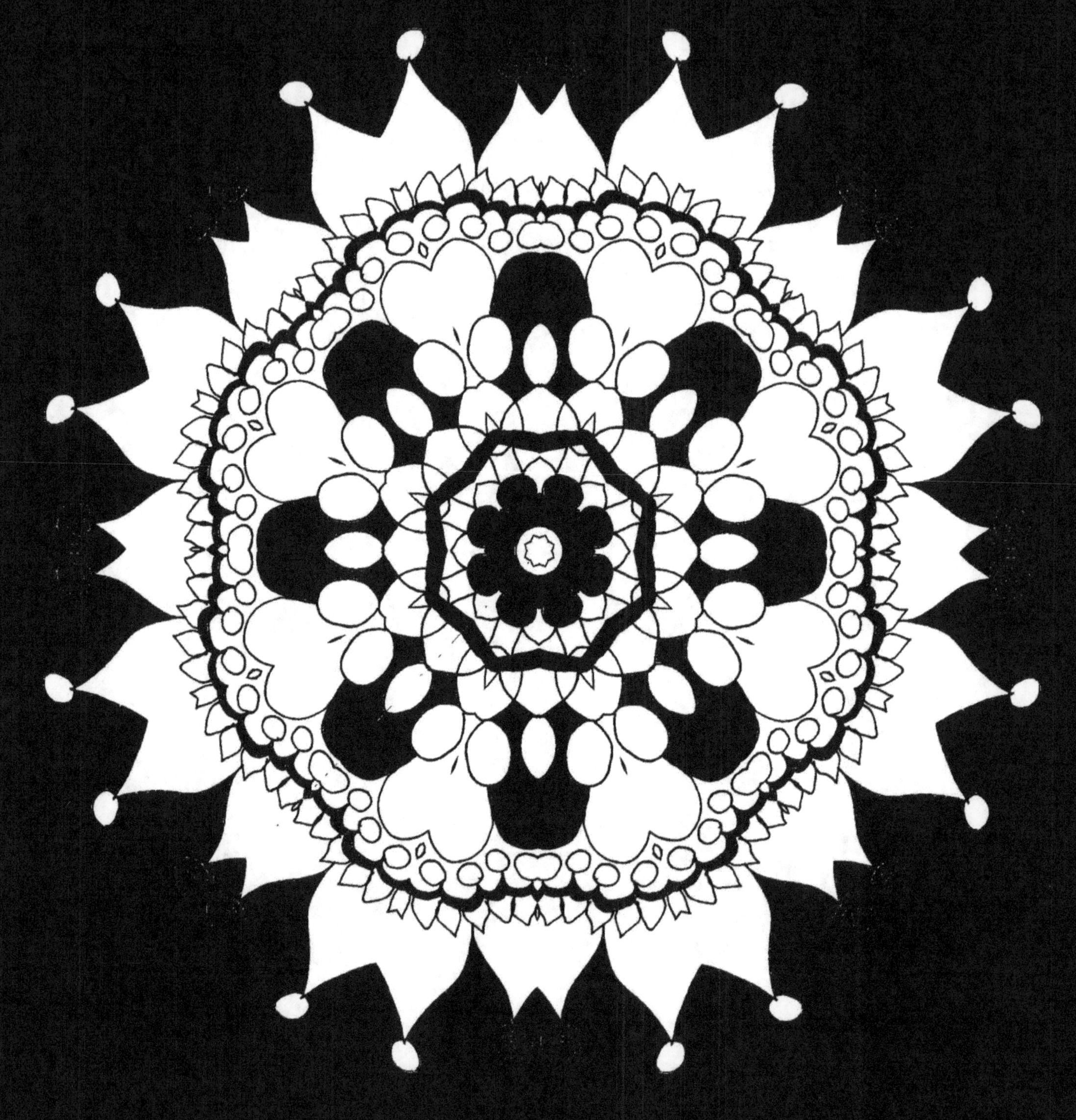

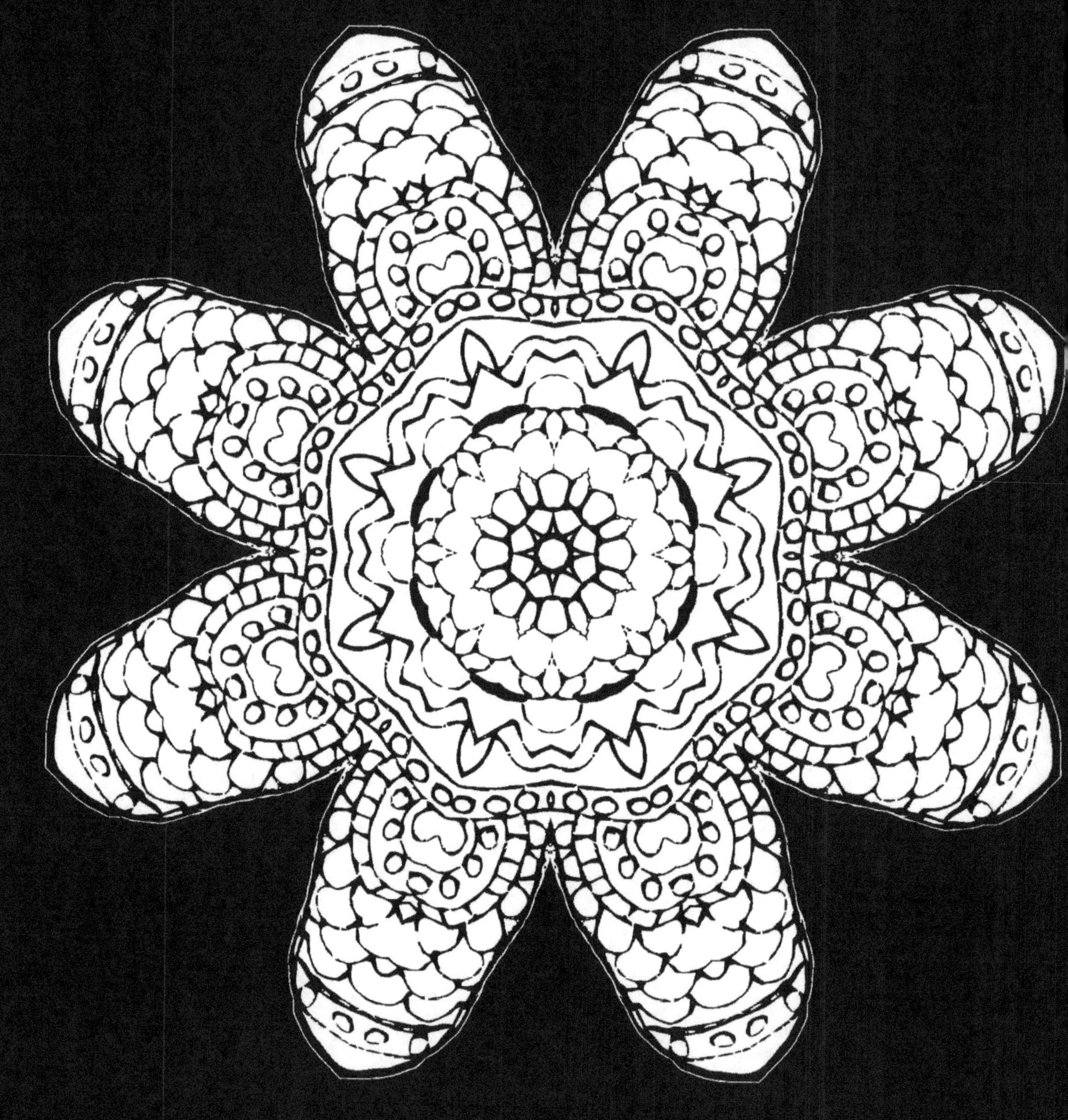

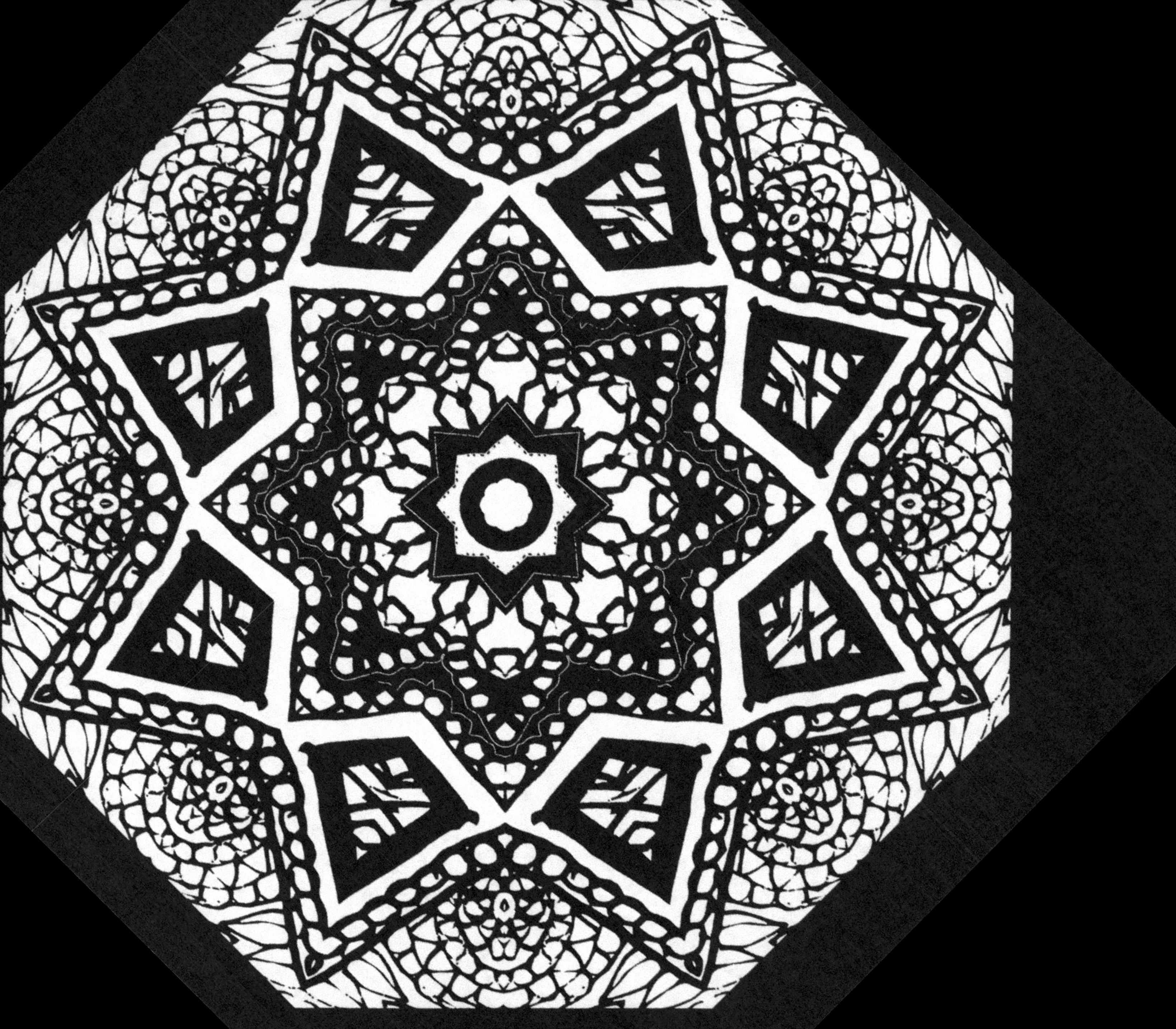

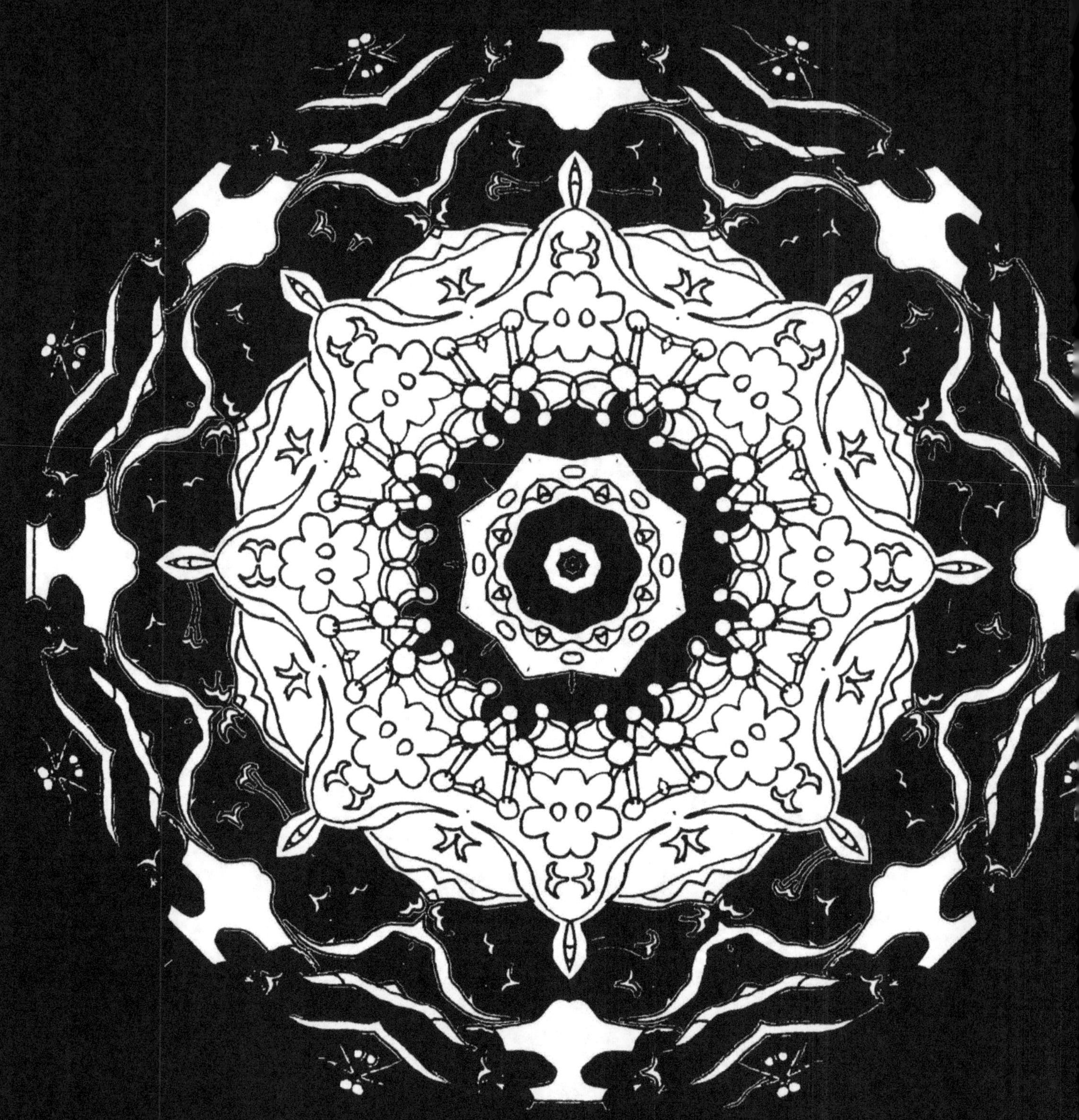

Thank you so much for purchasing this book! If you enjoyed it could you please leave a quick review on Amazon? I would really appreciate it. And it will help me a ton! I included some free regular Mandalas to color ☺ enjoy!!!

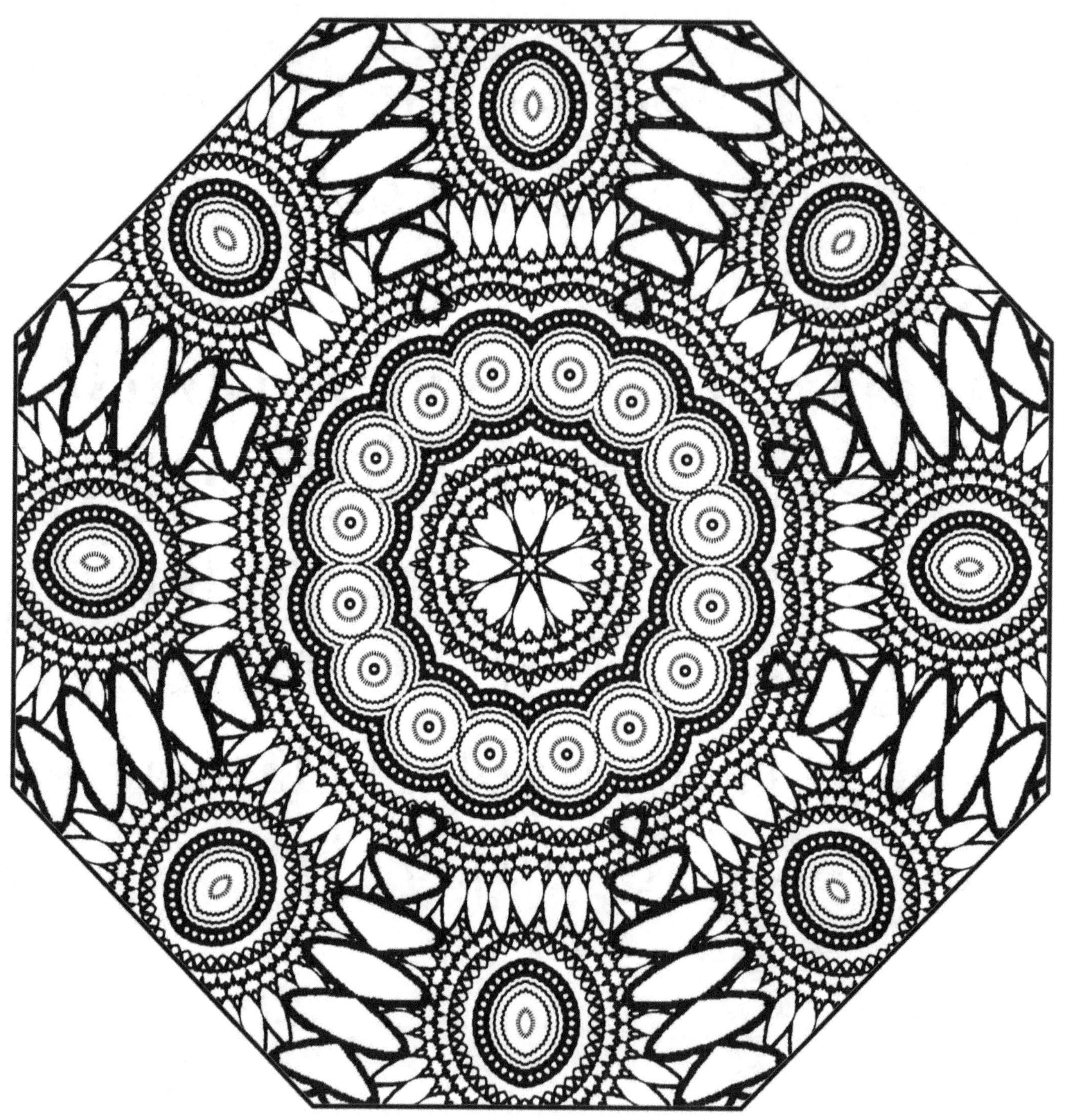

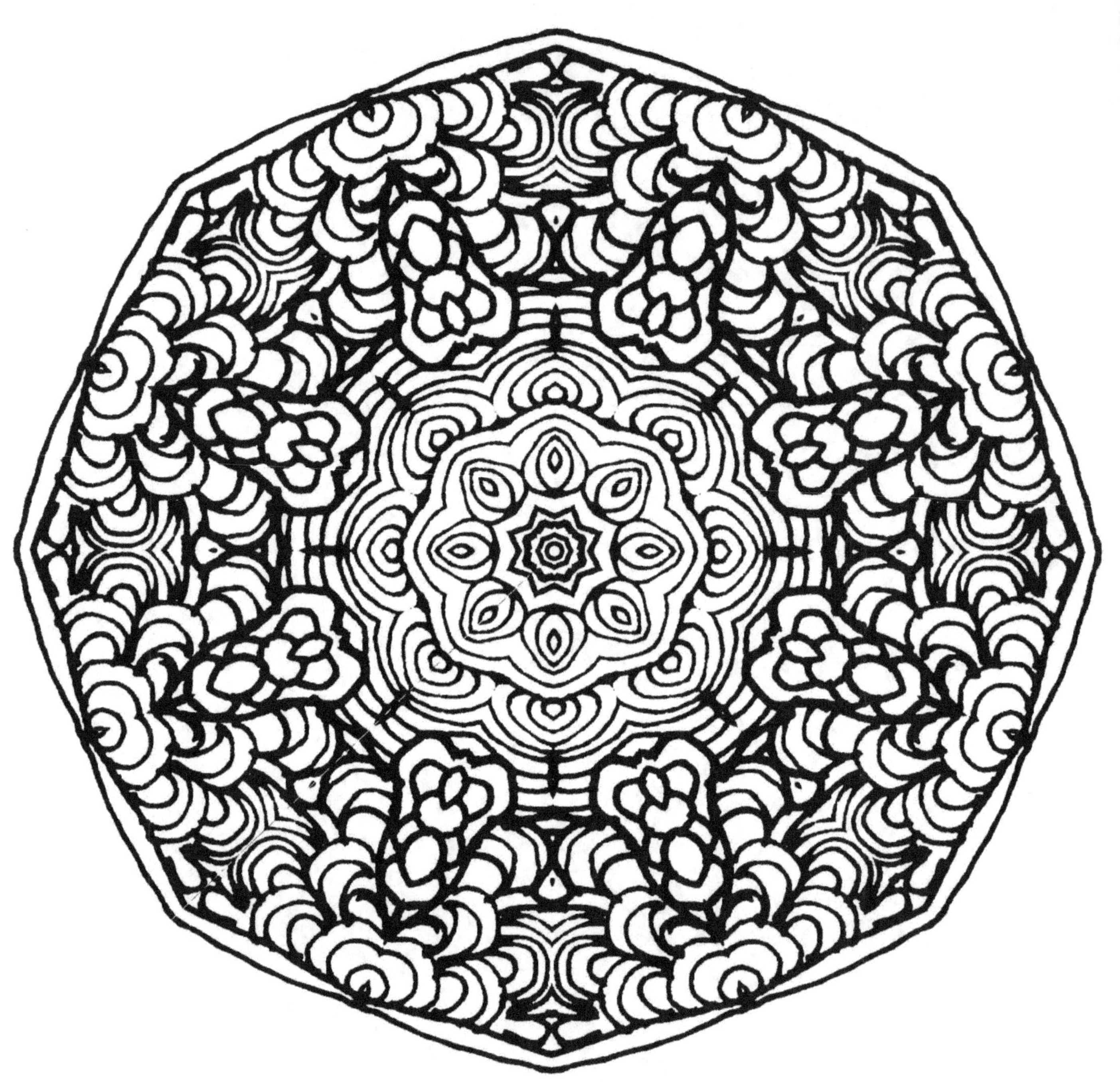

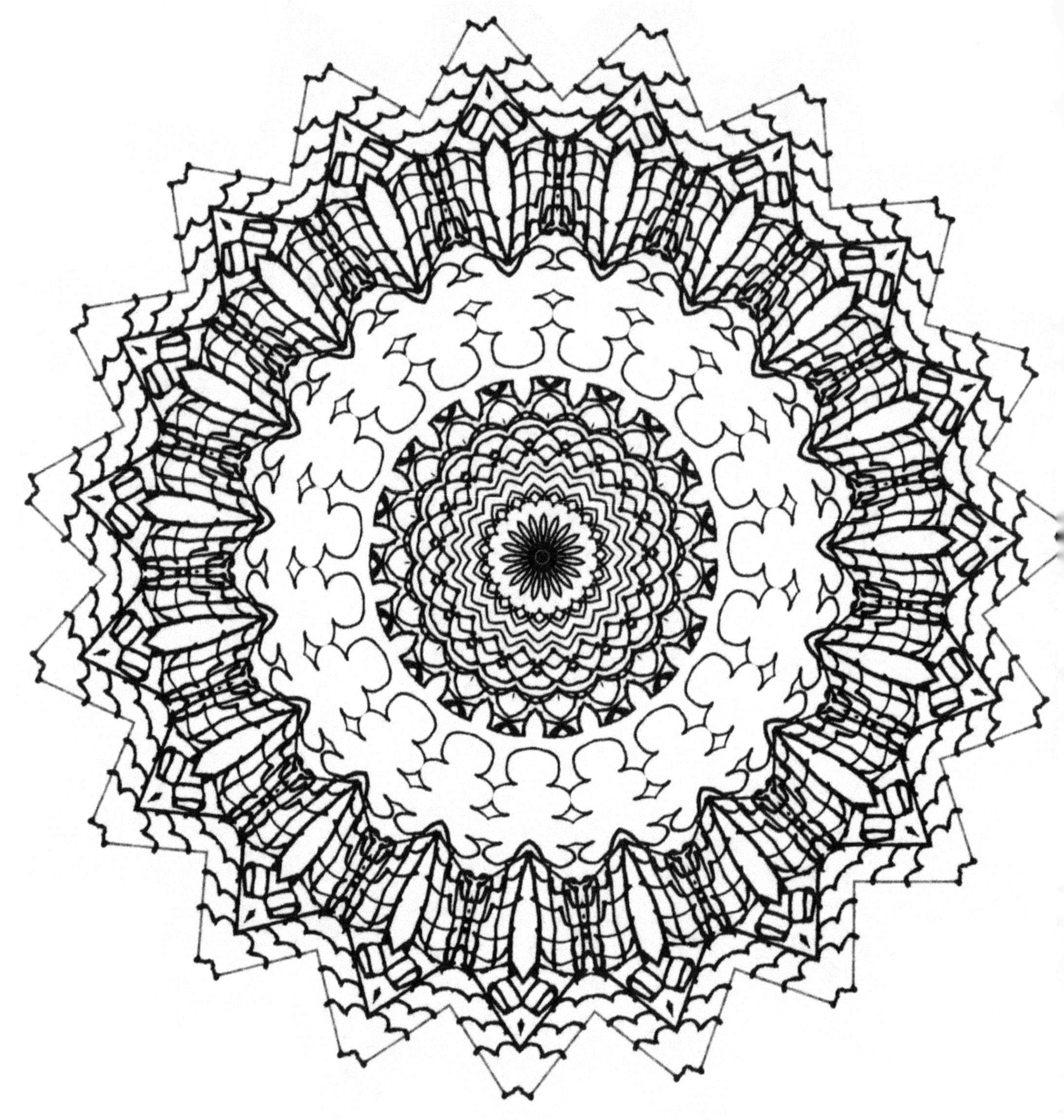